The Tiger's Eye, the Bird's Fist

The Tiger's Eye, The Bird's Fist

A Beginner's Guide to the Martial Arts

by Louise Rafkin

Illustrated by Leslie McGrath

Little, Brown and Company

Boston   New York   Toronto   London

FIRST EDITION

Front cover photograph: The House of Champions, Sensei Mark Parra. SGM: Brian Fong/Mario Prado.

Photography Credits

p. 4: Copyright British Museum; pp. 30 and 31: SGM: M. R. Prado; pp. 34 and 35: Archive Photos/Foto International; p. 36: Terry Lee; p. 41: Gon Buurman; p. 42: Lena Chow; p. 62: Stephen K. Hayes/Nine Gates; p. 69: Majan Ovesen; pp. 79, 106, and 112: SGM: Brian Fong/Mario Prado (The House of Champions/Sensei Mark Parra); pp. 114 and 115: by permission of Joseph T. Catlett Jr.; p. 119: Gon Buurman (left) Mike Duncan (right); p. 123: Archive Photos/New Line; p. 124: by permission of Michele "Mouse" Krasnoo.

Library of Congress Cataloging-in-Publication Data
Rafkin, Louise.
   The tiger's eye, the bird's fist : a beginner's guide to the martial arts /
by Louise Rafkin ; illustrated by Leslie McGrath. —1st ed.
     p.   cm.
   Includes bibliographical references and index.
   ISBN 0-316-73464-0
   1. Martial arts.   I. McGrath, Leslie.   II. Title.
GV1101.R34   1997
796.8 — dc20   96-35407

10 9 8 7 6 5 4 3 2 1

Q-HAW

Published simultaneously in Canada by Little, Brown & Company (Canada) Limited

PRINTED IN THE UNITED STATES OF AMERICA

For Ashley and Ryan

———

Author's Acknowledgments

I am indebted to the many writers and researchers who have compiled primary information about the history of the martial arts, and to those martial artists who took the time to talk with me about their training. I am enormously grateful to my teacher, Barbara Niggel, and to everyone I have "bowed in" with over the years. Each has given me the amazing opportunity to explore and refine my understanding of the martial arts, and most of all, myself.

Knowing others is intelligence; knowing yourself is true wisdom.

—Lao-tzu, TAO TE CHING

CONTENTS

—

Part One
EARLY HISTORY 1

Part Two
MARTIAL ARTS AROUND THE WORLD 27

Part Three
TRAINING TODAY   75

The *Dojo, Kwoon,* or School • Nighttime Adventure • The Bow • Meditation • Letting Go • The Story of the Okinawan Samurai • *Kata* Practice • Hand Strikes • Kicking Techniques • Stance Training • Blocks and Parries • A Million Times • *Kiai!* • The Legend of the Stone Tiger • Training Exercises • Christine Bannon-Rodriques • The Tests of the Shaolin Monks • Belts and Sashes • How Long? • Better than Okay • Ranking • Weapons • Advanced Training

Part Four
MARTIAL ARTS AND YOU   107

What's Right for You? • Tournaments • A Family Affair • Disabled Martial Artists • When to Fight, When Not to Fight • Self-Defense • Three Principles • A Modern Code of Honor • Samurai Self-Defense • Martial Arts in Film • Michele "Mouse" Krasnoo • The Wise Old Woman

Part One

—

EARLY HISTORY

—

What are the martial arts? Karate, judo, kung fu, aikido—what do these names mean? When we see strangely dressed people kicking, punching, and throwing each other to the ground, what are they actually doing?

Studying a martial art is a great way to get exercise and to get in shape. It is a way to learn respect for others and for yourself. Some arts teach amazing skills of self-defense. Others teach concentration and, above all else, focus. Training in the martial arts is all of this and more.

For the serious student, the martial arts are a way of life. The first martial artists trained not to be aggressive and warlike but to become better people through discipline and hard work. In addition to training, they spent their days meditating and studying philosophy. Spiritual people, their goal was to attain enlightenment. Enlightenment is difficult to put into words, but it is a feeling of oneness with the universe, as if everything in the world is just as it should be.

Training in a martial art means disciplining not just the body but the mind and the spirit as well. The martial arts are rooted in honor, respect, and the commitment to peace. Although many martial artists are highly skilled fighters, these underlying values make them different from street fighters and bullies. True martial artists are compassionate people who use their skills only to protect themselves or those they love.

FROM THE
ANIMALS

—

Fighting for survival dates back to the cave dwellers. The earliest people faced attack by wild animals, and in their search for food, they learned to look on these same animals as prey. Many of these animals were excellent fighters that used sharp fangs and claws as weapons. Many were faster than humans and instinctively able to anticipate their movements. For cave dwellers, staying alive meant being able to outsmart their animal attackers and prey. So, both to defend themselves and to better their hunting skills, they studied the animals' movements and strategies.

These people soon discovered that they were safer from attack and more effective hunters if they banded together in groups. As communities started to form, the clans laid claim to hunting territories. Soon, people were fighting with each other over land rights.

These early struggles of primitive peoples are the origins of fighting and warfare, but not of the martial arts. Although no one knows exactly how the martial arts began, many legends and stories explain the origins of these organized fighting styles.

One of the problems in studying the history of the martial arts is that the masters of the past were secretive about sharing their skills. Often, practices were held in private and students sworn to secrecy. At several points in history, the study of the martial arts went underground. Whole schools were hidden from society when governments, threatened by the idea of people learning the skills of hand-to-hand combat, outlawed the study of martial arts.

Most Asian martial artists trace the beginning of their arts to the legend of a traveling Indian monk.

Names and Terms

Many people think that the term *karate* refers to all the martial arts, but it is actually the specific name for the fighting arts of Okinawa. The word literally means "empty hand," referring to the fact that the art was originally performed without weapons. *Kempo* is a general word for Japanese martial arts, and American karate is often called *kenpo.*

Kung fu is a general expression for Chinese martial arts. It literally means "hard work," or something that takes a considerable time to learn. *Ch'uan fa,* which means "way of the fist," is the name for traditional Chinese fighting arts. In modern China, martial arts are referred to as *wushu,* the classical term for self-defense or military arts.

The Indonesian martial arts are called *pentjak silat.* Brazilians practice a dancelike martial art called *capoeira,* and the Koreans developed the high-kicking art of tae kwon do. Although we most often hear of karate and kung fu, many different arts are practiced around the world, each with its own name, character, and history.

Martial Arts Artifacts

Evidence indicates that martial arts have been around for many centuries. A five-thousand-year-old plaque found in Babylonia shows two figures in martial arts positions. Schools of archery opened in China over two thousand years ago. A book surviving from 700 B.C. tells us that fighting with fists was part of the regular education of young Chinese men between the ages of fifteen and twenty.

In the third century A.D., a Chinese doctor named Hua-t'o maintained that people needed to sweat and work up an appetite to be healthy. He developed exercises for good health based on the movements of five animals: the tiger, deer, bear, ape, and bird. Although these exercises were not fighting techniques, they led to the development of the Chinese martial arts.

THE STORY OF BODHIDHARMA

—

About fifteen hundred years ago, a monk named Bodhidharma left his home in India and headed to China. The long trip took Bodhidharma, alone and on foot, hundreds of miles through the snow-covered Himalaya Mountains. He navigated forests full of hidden bandits. He crossed swamps and rivers. Bodhidharma's purpose was to spread his new spiritual practice and philosophy, which would come to be called Zen Buddhism.

Bodhidharma had been born the son of a wealthy landowner, but as a young man he was restless and unfulfilled. For a while, hoping it would bring him happiness, he lived a luxurious life with many servants, rich food, and several wives. When that failed to satisfy him, he gave everything away and became a poor monk. Still, he was not at peace. Eventually he grew tired of the endless search for happiness and sat down under a tree. He vowed not to move until he found the meaning of life. He sat, and sat, and sat some more. After nine years of silent meditation, Bodhidharma finally found happiness and peace.

Bodhidharma believed that wisdom could be gained by sitting with oneself. He knew from his own experiences that money, possessions, and material gains didn't make one happy. Only by understanding oneself was there a possibility for peace and a deep sense of well-being. This feeling is called enlightenment by those who practice Buddhism.

This new Buddhism, which centered on meditation, would come to be called Ch'an by the Chinese and Zen by the Japanese. Bodhidharma is considered the father of Zen Buddhism. When he left his native India, his goal was to teach what he had learned to all who would listen.

Bodhidharma's destination was the Shaolin monastery, in what is now the Henan Province in China. The Shaolin monks were famous for their excellent translations of Buddhist scriptures. They spent hours poring over large books and scrolls, carefully choosing the best way to translate the holy words.

When Bodhidharma arrived, he tried to tell the monks that meditation was the ulti-mate spiritual practice. He urged them to put down their books and sit quietly, suggesting that enlightenment came from experiencing a clear mind. But the head of the monastery, threatened by Bodhidharma's teachings, ordered him to leave the temple. The monks went back to their books.

Bodhidharma retreated to a nearby cave and continued to meditate. Some say he began and ended each day with two hours of wall-gazing meditation. Though many thought he was a little crazy, eventually monks from the monastery and peasants from nearby villages came to see what was going on. They asked him questions, hoping to understand what he was doing. Bodhidharma spoke with nobody, yet his silence spoke volumes. His message was that words, spoken or written, were not the way to enlightenment. Unlike many other religions of the time, Bodhidharma's approach to Buddhism was accessible to everybody, both rich and poor, those who could read and those who could not read. Bodhidharma wanted everyone to look within themselves to find the truth. Gradually people began to meditate.

According to the story, after years of meditation, Bodhidharma's piercing blue eyes were so clear that they had burned a hole in the wall of his cave. The leader of the monastery could no longer deny that Bodhidharma had discovered something powerful. The doors of the Shaolin Temple were finally opened to his teachings.

SLEEPY MONKS

—

When you seek it, you cannot find it.
—Zen riddle

Bodhidharma began training the monks in meditation, emphasizing the importance of discipline and hard work. The monks were required to attend daily sessions of meditation, the first beginning in the early light of dawn. In addition to the difficult task of having to clear and focus the mind, meditation was hard on the body. The monks had been sitting at desks for many years, and their bodies were out of shape and tired. Many of the monks fell asleep in the meditation hall.

Based on his belief in the connection between body and soul, Bodhidharma realized that the body must be in shape in order to be spiritually fit. He began instructing the monks in training exercises similar to fighting movements he had learned in his homeland of India.

The exercises strengthened the monks' legs and gave them the energy to study and meditate. Bodhidharma taught the difficult movements after meditation sessions, when the monks were sore and stiff. Soon he added hand movements and body positions.

One such position was the horse stance. The student stood with legs wide, knees bent, and back straight as if riding a horse. While in the horse stance, the monks added punching movements and other self-defense moves. They became stronger and developed balance.

Sometimes the monks were asked to hold the horse stance for long peri-

ods, not moving even if they had an itch. Even when their legs burned and ached, they had to hold still. But by drawing on their new spiritual strength, they learned to overcome their bodies' limitations.

Likewise, the increased physical energy of the monks helped them to develop mental focus. Breathing deeply and fully, they taught themselves to calm their jumpy minds. Through meditation, they sought to be aware of and develop their life force, called *chi*. Working with *chi* is the basis of all martial arts. Without it, punches and kicks are merely physical motions lacking real energy.

As the monks became healthier, they were able to sit for longer periods of time. Their martial skills also developed. The first exercises taught by Bodhidharma at the Shaolin Temple were called the Eighteen Hands of the Lo Han, or Exercises for the Greatest Holiness. Many of the movements stressed speed over strength, which made it possible for men, women, and children of any size or age to become powerful and effective. The developing martial art was called Shaolin Ch'uan Fa, or the Way of the Shaolin Fist.

Shaolin Ch'uan Fa was used only in self-defense. The monks never started a fight and would use their skills only to defend themselves. After several years of daily practice, the Shaolin students became known for their fighting skills and fearless attitudes. Their sharpened minds were able to sense an attack before it even happened. Few dared to fight the quiet yet powerful monks. When one of the bands of thieves that roamed the countryside did attack the monastery, the monks stood strong and repelled the aggressors.

Often the students of the Shaolin Fist could avoid fighting altogether. They talked their way out of harmful situations or managed to escape. They never fought for money or to show off. The monks had learned well from their teacher. Bodhidharma taught that the best fighters never resorted to fighting. This belief in nonviolence is at the heart of martial arts training: The most skilled fighters are strong enough *not* to fight. In China, this philosophy is called *wu-te*, which is the combination of discipline, respect for others, and a quiet, humble belief in oneself.

Word of the new religion and martial art spread across China, and people from all over the country came to study at the Shaolin Temple. Until Bodhidharma came along, only soldiers studied warfare. Now experienced monks and nuns traveled through the country, spreading Zen Buddhism and teaching the new movements.

Bodhidharma and the Shaolin monks are responsible for bringing together the spiritual and physical threads of the martial arts. During his lifetime, Bodhidharma's teachings and exercises spread to Korea, Okinawa, and

Zen Buddhism

Those who know don't talk.
Those who talk don't know.
—Lao-tzu, TAO TE CHING

Zen is now practiced all over the world. Many martial arts schools follow the tradition of Bodhidharma and begin or end training sessions with periods of sitting meditation called *zazen*.

Zazen is done in perfect stillness. One sits cross-legged in a lotus position, each foot tucked up on the opposite leg, facing a blank wall. The back is straight; eyes are open only halfway. While sitting, one concentrates on following the breath in and out, in an attempt to quiet the mind. The goal is to let thoughts arise and flow right through one's mind in order to experience the present moment. This practice is much harder than it appears!

Anyone can meditate and may benefit from the discipline and mindfulness that comes as a result of "just sitting." Many students seek the calm that comes from quiet reflection. Others seek to strengthen the connection between their mind and body. Meditation also helps people understand themselves. As Pema Chodron, a Tibetan Buddhist nun, says, meditation is a way "to study ourselves and get to know ourselves now, not later."

Japan. Soon the arts traveled even farther—south and west to Burma, Thailand, Indonesia, and Malaysia. As the movements spread, they changed and developed according to the customs of each country and the terrain on which they were practiced. In rocky areas, low stances were practiced. In sandy areas, one-legged stances proved useful. In wetlands, techniques for fighting on soft or wet ground were developed.

Today a picture of Bodhidharma hangs in the training hall of many modern schools. In pictures, the old monk is ugly, with deep blue eyes, dark messy hair, and a full beard. We will never know whether this picture and the story of Bodhidharma is completely accurate.

A Single Sandal

According to legend, several attempts were made to poison Bodhidharma, but his chi, his life energy, was so strong that the poison did not affect him. It is said that Bodhidharma lived to be 150 years old. One story claims that after Bodhidharma's death and burial, he was spotted walking in the Onion Range in the mountains of Turkestan, carrying a single sandal. When asked where he was going, he replied, "I am going back to the Western Heaven," meaning India. The emperor was told that Bodhidharma had been seen alive and was so baffled that he ordered his grave dug up. And what was found? Just one sandal!

Training and Healing

Training at the Shaolin Temple was extremely difficult and frequently resulted in injuries. At one time or another, nearly every student suffered from pulled muscles, bruises, and even broken bones. But the Shaolin monks were trained to heal injuries, and some became skilled doctors. The monks studied massage and acupuncture, as well as traditional Chinese herbal remedies. Various plants eased sore muscles, and following the Shaolin tradition, today's martial artists usually learn massage as part of advanced training.

To win one hundred victories
in one hundred wars
is not the ultimate skill.
To stop the enemy without fighting
is the ultimate skill.
—Sun Tzu, THE ART OF WAR

LAO-TZU

—

Another figure important to the development of the martial arts is Lao-tzu. A teacher and philosopher born in the sixth century B.C., Lao-tzu taught that all living things should live in harmony with nature.

The symbol of Lao-tzu's teachings is the yin-yang. An ancient image, dating back more than three thousand years, the yin-yang symbol represents opposites working together in harmony. The wave of dark is the yang, which moves smoothly into the wave of light, the yin. A dot of each, dark and light, is in the other, so the design is perfectly balanced. Yang is considered hard, and yin soft. Yin and yang are also viewed in the natural world as day and night, positive and negative, birth and death, and hot and cold. This list of opposites can go on forever.

Lao-tzu taught his students that yin and yang are the principles of nature. This philosophy of all things working together came to be known as Taoism.

Harmonizing with the natural flow of energy in the world is at the heart of a martial artist's training.

"The softest thing in the world can overcome the hardest thing in the world," Lao-tzu wrote. He was referring to the way that a constant stream of water can wear away even the biggest boulder. Water flows under, over, or around, in order to keep moving on its path. You can easily put your hand into water, and it will give way. But an ocean wave can just as easily knock you over! Water takes many forms: ice, steam, and liquid. Water is needed by all living things. It is hard and soft, powerful and yielding. Because of its great power in the natural world, many martial arts disciplines use water in the symbols of their styles.

Lao-tzu's words are collected in a book of poems called the *Tao Te Ching*, which means The Book of the Way. This book is widely read today by people of many religions. Nearly fifty English translations have been made of it, and more than a hundred books have been written about it in Chinese.

The Story of Chang San-feng

Chang San-feng, the founder of the art of t'ai chi, was a hermit who lived by himself in the mountains during the fourteenth century. He spent his whole life training and studying Taoism. Legends claim that he was over seven feet tall, with the bones of a crane and the body of a pine tree. A lover of nature, he often practiced t'ai chi in the moonlight. Practice in the dark increased his awareness and developed his energy. Each night, he meditated at midnight. It is said that he could walk on snow without leaving a footprint. His closest companions were a tiger and a crane.

Once while walking in the forest, Chang San-feng ran into some members of the royal family on a hunting expedition. Thinking Chang San-feng was a beggar, they ordered him out of their way. Chang San-feng smiled. "You use bow and arrow to hunt; I use only my hands," he said. Reaching into the air, he caught two hawks flying overhead. "I don't want to hurt them," he said, letting them go free. "I respect all living things."

One of the princes became angry. Grabbing an arrow from his sheath, he shot at Chang San-feng. Chang San-feng simply opened his mouth and caught the arrow between his teeth. Then he threw the arrow at a tree with such power that it stuck deeply in the bark. "I have no need for violent weapons," he said.

The royal hunting party realized that they had met a supernaturally powerful man. They abandoned their hunt and left the forest in a hurry.

CHI

—

Chi is the Chinese word for the breath of life. It is more than the inhaling and exhaling of air, however. It is energy. Everything in the universe has *chi:* people, animals, the wind, even plants.

The center of *chi* in the body is just a few inches below the belly button and is called the *tan-tien* or the *hara. Chi* is sometimes compared to blood because it pulses through the body. Yet the Chinese believe that instead of traveling through veins, *chi* flows through the body on energy paths called meridians. These meridians must be free from blocks in order to let the *chi* flow smoothly. Exercises for *chi* development help to keep the meridians clear.

Chi kung is an art devoted to building *chi* for healing and good health. Its forms include controlled breathing and focused concentration, and it has been practiced for more than two thousand years in China. The art of *chi kung* is now spreading to other parts of the world. People with a variety of illnesses, such as cancer, HIV, allergies, and arthritis, have responded positively to *chi kung* exercises and treatments.

Acupuncture is another Chinese healing art; it uses needles to direct and increase the flow of *chi* in the body. Although sticking needles into the body may seem primitive, acupuncture is a respected healing practice that was developed more than five thousand years ago.

Chi can be released in a forceful way, with a fast punch or a kick, or it can flow as one breathes, smoothly and slowly. Many training exercises strengthen the *chi* center, in order to focus the balance of the body in this area. The Chinese also believe that *chi* is affected by food and sub-scribe to diets that enhance *chi* development.

Because *chi* is not a physical attribute, both men and women of all sizes can develop great *chi* power. In a fight, a muscle-bound man with little *chi* will lose out to a small woman who has developed *chi*. Women depend on internal power more than brute strength, so their *chi* often develops faster and stronger than does that of their fellow male students.

One story about the power of *chi* tells of the master Yang-Lu-chu-an. While sitting in meditation, Yang-Lu-chu-an was approached by a visitor, apparently come to pay his respects. Suddenly the visitor attacked with both fists! The master is said to have moved slightly and barely touched the man's fist with his arm to block the strike. But such was the power of Yang-Lu-chu-an's *chi* that the man flew across the room as if he had been hit by lightning.

Belief in the existence and power of an internal energy is worldwide. In China, one can witness demonstrations of *chi* power in public parks, where in early mornings the masters practice with their students. A quiet touch from a master with *chi* power can send a student quickly tumbling backward. Weightlifters use *chi* power, as do opera singers. Both are skilled in using breath to focus their skills. People who study yoga use *chi*, which they call *prana*. In Japan, this internal energy is called *ki*. In Indonesia, where martial artists are also healers, *chi*, called *ilmu*, is often focused in the palms. A recent film documentary showed an Indonesian master starting a fire simply by placing his hand over a crumpled piece of paper.

Most people have used *chi* power without realizing they have done so. You may have drawn on this energy if you have been extremely scared or in danger. By breathing deeply before a test or other nerve-racking event, you are using and developing this internal power.

ANIMALS AT PLAY AND AT WAR

—

Over the centuries, martial artists have devoted years to the study of wild creatures, from small insects to large beasts. They watched how animals fought and noted which strategies were most effective, then copied these movements. These age-old styles are still popular today and include the movements of animals and insects as diverse as the tiger, snake, crane, and praying mantis.

The tiger approaches silently and slowly, then pounces with great force. This powerful animal is a difficult opponent, especially on slippery or wet ground, where its low body position gives it more stability. Tiger stylists learn to stalk, waiting for their moment; to leap and strike with strength; and to move swiftly and powerfully on the ground. In addition, the tiger claw is a dangerous martial technique, used to scratch and gouge the face and neck.

The snake is often copied for its ability to strike rapidly from any position. Just as a snake takes down its prey with one fast and furious attack, snake stylists are quick and deadly. Sometimes the hands strike from the cobra position, with the thumb and forefinger extended like fangs, targeting the throat or eyes.

The crane is often imitated in martial arts forms. It has inspired the one-legged stances, as well as hopping movements, patterned after the way these beautiful birds flit gracefully over rough ground, from rock to rock, or

through shallow water. Other crane forms include high kicks from one-legged stances and fast arm motions that mimic the flutter of beating wings. Striking with the fingers out straight and tightly together is called a bird's fist. This hand technique is used to peck the eyes or the head.

The tiny praying mantis, a remarkably beautiful and delicate insect, has been the inspiration for a number of martial arts styles. This insect blends into the background of the leaves and bark on which it sits. Then, suddenly, without any warning, the praying mantis strikes with such force and accuracy that it captures its prey with one movement. Praying mantis stylists practice standing perfectly still and then plucking a fly from the air with a pair of chopsticks!

Many martial arts copy the movements of the monkey. One story claims that the first monkey forms were developed by a man who was unfairly jailed by the Manchus, a race of foreigners who ruled China for several centuries. According to the story, the Manchus used apes as prison guards. For more than ten years, the prisoner watched the apes from his cell. He saw how they fought, hunted, and played. In order to keep in shape, the man copied the apes' movements and hunting techniques. When he was finally released, he came to be known as the Monkey Master.

There are many kinds of monkey movements. The small chimpanzees roll and fall, playing, and circling their opponents. Fighting a monkey stylist, one might get confused or dizzy trying to follow all the circling. A monkey fighter will use trickery and try to catch his or her opponent off guard.

Some styles copy the movements of the drunken monkey. In the jungles, monkeys sometimes feed on fruit that has spoiled in the hot weather of the tropical climates, and they become drunk on the fermented juice. These drunken monkeys look silly, falling and stumbling about. But, if provoked, they will fight fiercely.

Students of the drunken monkey act out a fake drunkenness. The martial artist reels around, looking out of control. But the student is able to snap out of the movement at any time with strong strikes. The opponent may relax, thinking he is fighting a drunken fool. Perhaps the fight will not even take place because the attacker might think it stupid to fight a drunk. However, if he goes ahead with his attack, he will be surprised by the drunken monkey's quick change of mood.

Other martial arts movements come from the deer, the leopard, the lion, and the mythical fire-breathing dragon, which the Chinese consider to be a spiritual and extremely powerful creature. To fight with the spirit of the dragon is an ultimate challenge.

The Legend of Shuen Guan

According to legend, at thirteen years old, the young girl Shuen Guan was such an excellent fighter that she was called the Little Tigress.

When Shuen Guan's town was attacked by thieves, she was the only person brave enough to fight them, finally slipping past the enemy and running to alert some soldiers camped nearby. The leader of the soldiers was so impressed by Shuen Guan's skill and bravery that they went back to the town with her and fought the thieves side by side. The town was saved, and the Little Tigress was honored by the people of her town as well as by the emperor of China.

SECRET STUDIES

—

For many centuries, the Shaolin Temple remained the center of martial arts study. By the 1600s, several thousand monks practiced in the temple courtyard. Skilled in bare-handed techniques, they also wielded swords, daggers, knives, and other more exotic weapons.

In the late 1600s, China was invaded by the Manchus, foreigners from the north. In order to avoid being arrested, Chinese officials and their supporters fled to the monasteries to hide. After shaving their heads, the officials were successfully disguised among the monks and nuns. Behind the temple and monastery walls they made plans to overthrow the invaders.

Eventually the Manchus found the hidden officials and discovered their secret plans. They mounted attacks, including one in which the Shaolin Temple was set on fire and burned to the ground. Those that managed to escape fled to the hills and went into hiding. The refugees of the Shaolin Temple traveled secretly to country villages, trying to gather support against the Manchus. They

sought to win back their country and their freedom.

For more than three hundred years, the Chinese people tried to fight the Manchus but were never victorious. The Manchus comprised only two percent of the population, yet they ruled over the Chinese majority with an iron fist. In 1730, they passed a law forbidding anyone to practice or teach martial arts, thinking this would prevent the Chinese from using their strong fighting skills against them. From the outside it looked as though all martial arts had suddenly disappeared.

However, the study of martial arts was too ingrained in Chinese society to be wiped out. People were secretly practicing at night, in the tall fields, and even in caves. Some martial artists joined the Peking Opera, a colorful circuslike group of skilled actors, musicians, and performers. At the opera, martial arts skills were disguised as acrobatics. In this way, the arts remained strong and were passed on despite the ban against training.

This public ban on training makes it difficult to trace the history of the arts. There are few written records of training exercises and little evidence of formal schools. However, by the early 1900s, when China was invaded by westerners seeking tea and other resources, there was still a strong martial arts under-

ground. Under attack from a common enemy, martial artists came out of hiding and fought alongside the Manchus against the western foreigners. This famous battle was called the Boxer Rebellion because the westerners, seeing the Chinese fighters kick and punch, thought they were up against boxers. Most Chinese fought hand to hand, even though the western powers freely used guns.

Unfortunately, the "boxers" were defeated by the western forces, and the remaining Manchus quickly turned against the martial artists who had helped them in their struggle. The Manchu empress executed many masters, closed the training halls, and once again outlawed the practice of martial arts.

ADAPTATION

—

Du|ring the centuries of war, martial arts were taught only to people who would protect the villagers against the foreign invaders. The masters were choosy about who they took on as students. In the wrong hands, martial skills could be deadly.

Underground groups of martial artists banded together in secret societies. One of the oldest secret societies was the Carnation Eyebrow Rebels. This group was powerful and always fought for good and fair government. Other groups were the White Lotus Society and Three Incense Sticks. Each society practiced its own style of martial arts.

As the study of martial arts spread throughout China, both openly and underground, each master changed and modified movements and added new ones. These emerging styles were usually named after the masters who taught them. Often the arts changed in ways that greatly helped the people who needed them most.

For instance, the southern Chinese fishermen needed ways to defend themselves against pirates who boarded their boats and stole their catches. In order to fight in a rocking boat, the men needed low, stable stances. And since it was impossible to use high kicks in a rough sea, kicking was used less often than strong hand strikes.

Since territory in northern China was rugged and sometimes icy, styles that developed in the north used rolling, falling, and jumping. The northerners had to be able to move quickly over uneven ground. Because people covered their hands in cloth to protect them from the cold, kicking was emphasized more than fist techniques. Those training on flat, open ground used jumping kicks and leg sweeps.

Every master had a different body type. Some were male, some female. Some were tall, others short, some heavy and some thin. Yet the good masters passed on their arts carefully. Although some adaptation of techniques occurred because of terrain and other factors, the masters who passed on only the techniques that worked with their bodies were not considered responsible. If each master changed the art to suit himself, the arts would soon be weakened and watered down. Rather, the true master taught pure techniques and then capitalized on developing his own strengths and those of his students.

Always in history, those who loved fighting were destroyed,
But those who didn't know how to fight were also destroyed.
Goodness and strength will last and can lead others
down the right path.
—Haukin Song of Meditation

JAPANESE ARTS
The Dip of the Sword

—

According to legend, Japan was created when the gods Izanagi and Izanami dipped their jeweled sword into the sea. As they drew the weapon from the water, four drops slipped off the edge of the blade. These drops became the four main islands of Japan.

For many centuries, the people who settled these islands lived peacefully. But in the seventh century, changes in the government created trouble. In a struggle for land, family groups, called clans, began to fight with each other. To protect their families, warriors from each clan fought hard and without fear. These fighters were known as the samurai, which means "those who serve." For several hundred years, Japanese samurai from various clans fought countless battles. There was so much strife that one period, between 1490 and 1600, is called the Age of the Country at War.

On horseback, in a decorated suit of scaled armor bound together by colorful leather laces, the samurai was a formidable figure. His long ponytail, called a topknot, sprung from a hole in his metal helmet. Swinging swords, daggers, and the *naginata*, a heavy knifelike weapon that could be up to four feet long, the samurai were proud of their skills with bladed weaponry. The samurai's sword was so sharp that it could easily slice through the metal of his enemies' armor. It could also slice a European sword as easily as a piece of meat. The famous sword maker Kanemoto II

created a sword so strong that it could cut a gun barrel in two.

Strict rules governed the handling of a samurai's sword. No one was allowed to touch another person's weapon. When visiting a friend, the samurai had to leave his sword outside in order to show his goodwill. Treated with respect and honor, swords were handed down from father to son.

As warriors of the ruling lords, samurai often fought fiercely and to the death over the rights to land and property. Yet the samurai were educated, spiritual men who followed a strict code of ethics and were students of Zen Buddhism and its practices. Meditation helped them develop the discipline and focus to go forward into battle without fear. The highest goal of the samurai was to charge into battle without thinking of the outcome. To die in battle was considered honorable.

It was traditional for samurai to write poems before going into battle. They studied flower arranging and were versed in the refined Zen ritual of the tea ceremony. Comprising a simple room, the tea house contained a single flower arrangement, a scroll with a poem in Japanese calligraphy, tea bowls, and tea utensils. The samurai left his sword and shoes outside the tea house and once inside, sought to calm his mind. The tea ceremony reminded the samurai of the beauty, simplicity, and shortness of life.

Interclan fighting had created the samurai, but these warriors soon faced a common enemy. When the Mongols attacked Japan in the thirteenth century, the samurai fought bravely but lost. After retreating, they were shocked to find that their enemy had killed not only warriors but also women, children, and older people. These foreigners had weapons that the samurai had never seen: bamboo poles that flung rocks. But the samurai decided to fight again quickly before the foreigners brought more weapons and soldiers. This time they stood their ground. The samurai fought with their razor-sharp swords.

When faced with a third invasion, the devout samurai sought the help of their religious leaders. Just as the invading force reached the islands, a strong wind blew in and destroyed their ships. The samurai called this wind *kamikaze,* translated as "holy wind," because they believed it had been sent by the gods to help them.

Once peace fell on the islands, the samurai started to train in the spiritual side of swordsmanship. Peacetime gave the warriors time to refocus, and they began to develop their internal powers. A new school of training developed. Called the New Shade school, this mental training taught the warrior to keep his mind hidden from his enemy. The goal was to be aware, but cloaked, as if a shade were drawn over the mind.

The founder of this school, Kamiizumi Hidetsuna, once saved a young girl who had been kidnapped by a madman. Dressed in the robes of a monk, Hidetsuna offered rice cakes to both the child and her kidnapper. When the man reached for the cake, Hidetsuna leapt forward and rescued the child. The monk whose robes Hidetsuna had borrowed was so impressed by this strategy of deception that he offered his holy robes as a gift.

CHOISAI SENSEI

Violence, even well intentioned, always rebounds upon oneself.
—Lao-tzu, TAO TE CHING

A great teacher of swordsmanship, Choisai Sensei lived in fifteenth-century Tokyo (*sensei* is a title of honor meaning "teacher" in Japanese). As a young samurai, Choisai took part in many battles. Having seen so much death, he knew that fighting led only to destruction for both the warrior and his family. He decided to find a new philosophical approach to fighting, so he spent one thousand days training and meditating. At the end of this time, he announced his new ideas about the samurai spirit. Choisai Sensei came to believe that a strong body was not a samurai's most important asset.

"We will come to realize that to win by cutting down our opponent is not a true victory. This is the meaning of peace," said Master Otake, a teacher of Choisai Sensei's art and philosophy. "If strength were the only thing, the animals that depend completely on power for survival, such as lions and tigers, would continue to increase and fill up the world. This is not the case. It is necessary for us to grasp a higher form of human wisdom and keep our brute power hidden."

As a famous warrior, Choisai Sensei was often challenged to fight. He would agree to fight but suggest that he and his opponent sit together first. Choisai Sensei would then climb onto a thin bamboo mat hanging several feet from the ground and settle softly on this precarious perch. The bamboo never collapsed under him. Motioning to the challenger to join him on the mat, the *sensei* seemed to be able to float on air. According to stories, when the opponents saw this great power, they decided not to fight. Instead, Choisai Sensei joined them for a cup of tea.

Part Two

—

Martial Arts Around the World

—

Today more than four hundred styles of martial arts are thriving in China alone. Japan and Okinawa boast many more. As the martial arts fanned out across Asia, styles developed and changed.

Americans were introduced to martial arts after World War II, when servicemen who had been stationed in Japan returned home full of enthusiasm for karate. As Asian countries opened to the west, people from Japan and China moved to America and the arts became accessible to westerners. Meanwhile, martial artists in South America and Indonesia started revealing more about their once secretive arts.

Hundreds of styles of karate, kung fu, and other martial arts are now taught in the United States. Some styles have been handed down for generations and look much the same today as they did years ago. Other styles, such as the Hawaiian-American art of *kajukenbo*, have been created in the United States by masters from different countries who have worked together.

Each art has its own history and tradition. However, most arts share the goals of peace and spiritual development. The samurai had a name for this philosophy: Bushido. *Bu* is made up of two characters, the first meaning "to stop," the second meaning "spear." *Do* means "the way." So Bushido, the way of the warrior, literally means "the way to stop the spear." All true martial artists strive for peace, both for themselves and for the world.

So many martial arts are practiced today that it would be impossible to describe them all. The following pages highlight those arts that are best known and easily available to study, along with those that are more traditional and important in their homelands.

WUSHU

H igh-flying kicks and flashy techniques are the hallmarks of *wushu,* the official martial art form of Communist China. *Wushu* students are flexible and skilled in gymnastics. In addition to the athletic empty hand forms, the art of *wushu* includes the study of a wide range of weapons, including the whip chain and sword.

In China, schoolchildren, workers, university students, and many others practice *wushu* daily. If a child shows great skill, he or she might be enrolled at a government school and trained for the national team. *Wushu* athletes tour the world impressing westerners with their grace and excellence. *Wushu* demonstrations include amazing feats of physical power such as breaking boards, smashing bricks of ice, and lying on beds of nails.

WOODY WONG, WUSHU CHAMPION

One of the highest-ranking *wushu* competitors in the United States, Woody Wong began training at the age of twenty under Sifu Eric Chen and Sifu Liu Yu. An outstanding athlete, he has been on the United States *wushu* team three times.

When Woody was growing up, in Los Angeles's Chinatown, his father would take him to see Hong Kong–made kung fu movies. He was amazed by the superhuman feats of strength, agility, and courage on the big screen. Afterward, he and his father would go to a cafe for a late-night snack of chicken porridge topped with peanuts, followed by Chinese donuts.

Over the hot porridge, Wong's dad told him stories about the legendary heroes of the Shaolin Temple and explained *chi*, internal power used by Chinese martial arts masters. "Dad would get very animated," Woody recalls. "He used his left hand to show a slow circular block and then he would quickly execute a lethal palm strike to his right. His eyes squinted and then became bright and piercing. Even though my father never studied martial arts, I felt happy and proud when he told these tales of martial arts heroes. I asked him to tell me the same stories over and over again."

Later, after Wong had won many *wushu* championships, strangers would ask him how he did those acrobatic, aerial techniques. "I told them I watched a lot of kung fu flicks as a kid."

Wong attributes his success to three things: practice, good teachers, and persistence. "When I see someone do something better than me, I don't feel sorry for myself and I don't put the other person down," he says. "Instead I say, 'If he can do it, so can I.' And then I practice." He admits that sometimes practice is boring, but he realizes that how he practices is how he will perform.

Wong credits his trusting relationship with his Chinese teachers as being important to his success. "I respect these men and listen to their advice," he explains. "They have helped me so much and have given me so much of their time and insight that I try not to let them down."

And what about persistence? "Never, ever quit," he says. "Even when I had little confidence, my teachers expressed confidence in me. It is important to find a teacher who really has the heart to want to teach you—one who really cares."

The Story of the Chinese Lion Dance

Once upon a time, a wild lion snuck into a Chinese village. Snarling and growling, the lion scared the villagers, and they jumped back in fear. Though frightened, they sought to catch the wild beast. After a long struggle, the lion was finally trapped and beheaded.

When the lion got to heaven, the goddess of mercy felt sorry for the poor headless animal. So she used her red silk scarf to tie its head back onto its body. Then, in order to prevent further harm from befalling the beast, she put a magic mirror, which had the power to keep away evil, on its head.

Now the lion is said to bring good fortune and keep away bad luck. The colorful and humorous lion dance is performed at Chinese New Year events and other special occasions. The performers under the costume are kung fu or *wushu* students who have practiced the specialized movements of the lion. Observers see a wild, leaping lion and only glimpse the legs of the martial artists moving from stance to stance.

According to tradition, the longer the beard of the lion, the older the martial arts school. Lion dance competitions take place around the world. A good lion dance will reflect the cooperation and hard work of the students.

Wing Chun

With its focus on speed and economy of movement, the Chinese art of Wing Chun kung fu can be practiced by people of any size. Wing Chun is strong in self-defense applications; a skilled Wing Chun fighter, for example, can throw a deadly punch from the distance of only several inches. Called the three-to-one punch, this was Bruce Lee's signature technique. Few people know that the art that made Bruce Lee famous was developed by a Buddhist nun at the Shaolin monastery more than three hundred years ago.

A young nun named Ng Mui felt she needed to learn a martial art that could be effective for someone her size. She was small and light, and she knew that even her hardest punches could not do much against a big, heavy man. Through practice, she learned that her real strength was in speed. She was flexible and could strike quickly. Ng Mui's strikes were known to be as fast and sharp as the snap of a whip.

Whenever someone developed a new art, it was necessary for the master to prove its worth by accepting challenges from other martial artists. Ng Mui used her skills successfully against many masters of her day. She became famous and attracted many students, mostly women.

It is told that about this time, a pretty young woman, Yim Wing Chun, whose name means "beautiful spring-time," was being pressured by a wealthy but evil man to marry him against her will. Wing Chun was already engaged to a young man whom she loved but who lived in another province. The rich man insisted that Wing Chun's father break the engagement. Wing Chun was miserable and scared.

Ng Mui heard about Wing Chun's problem. She convinced the rich man that he should allow Wing Chun a year before forcing her to marry him. After all, it would take nearly that long for a letter to reach Wing Chun's fiancé and inform him of her new plans. The rich man agreed to wait.

Ng Mui began to teach Wing Chun how to fight. Wing Chun was an outstanding student, and Ng Mui soon taught her everything she knew. When the year was up, Ng Mui came up with a plan to solve Wing Chun's dilemma. She would tell the wealthy troublemaker that Wing Chun had been trained in karate as a child and was only allowed to marry someone who could beat her in a fight.

As Ng Mui had expected, the man was certain that he could defeat the delicate Wing Chun. The match was arranged.

Right off, the man charged at Wing Chun, but instantly she blocked his strikes and knocked him down. He rose and came at her again. Wing Chun hit harder and moved faster. After several more attempts, the man found that his strength and size did not match Wing Chun's technique and training. Finally he retreated and agreed to leave her alone.

Wing Chun continued to study with Ng Mui, and she married her original fiancé. When Ng Mui died, Yim Wing Chun carried on teaching the art that soon carried her name and that several hundred years later was taught to the most famous martial artist of modern times, Bruce Lee.

BRUCE LEE

Even compared to today's action heroes, Bruce Lee is still the world's most famous martial arts movie star. In 1958, Lee was a college student living in Seattle, Washington. There, he first started teaching westerners the Chinese martial arts he had studied since the age of eleven while growing up in Hong Kong. A skilled fighter, Lee had first been trained in Wing Chun, yet over the years, he began to develop his own style, which he called *jeet kune do*, or the "art of the intercepting fist."

Lee was a small man, standing only five feet eight inches tall and weighing 145 pounds. An ambitious person, he was challenged by many who questioned both his abilities and the merits of his style, but he never let such people stop him. Often pushing himself to the limit, Lee set high goals for himself. In 1964, at an International Tournament in California, he went hand to hand with the top fighters of his time in order to prove the worthiness of his art. He impressed many people and landed himself a role on *The Green Hornet*, a television action show.

His role as Kato, the central character's bodyguard, introduced Lee to millions of Americans. Even though the program lasted only a year and the role required him to wear a mask that disguised his Asian features, Lee collected a huge group of fans.

Lee stayed in Hollywood, teaching his art and trying to break into the movies. Life was difficult for him. He took a lot of criticism for teaching Chinese arts to westerners. And he found that being Chinese in Hollywood was not easy. The lead role in *Kung Fu*, the television show that introduced the philosophy of the martial arts and story of the Shaolin Temple to millions of Americans, was created for Lee. When the part went to a Caucasian actor, David Carridine, Lee was shocked and disappointed. *Kung Fu* soon became the most watched television program in the country.

Despite this setback, Lee pushed himself, training for hours at a time with a wooden dummy to increase his speed and accuracy. His fighting skills were legendary, and he became known as the Little Dragon. Discouraged with his progress in Hollywood, Lee went to Thailand to make his first movie, *The Big Boss*. Next was *Return of the Dragon*, which featured a fight scene between Lee and the new action star Chuck Norris.

Lee's big break, however, came when he made *Enter the Dragon*. Hollywood promoted the film all over the world, and Lee was finally acknowledged as a superstar.

In 1973, not long after his rise to fame, Lee died suddenly at the age of thirty-two during the filming of *Game of Death*. Although the death certificate cites brain swelling as the cause, some mystery remains about the circumstances of this tragedy. Some people claim that Lee was murdered by rival martial artists who didn't like his flashy Hollywood ways or his teaching martial arts to non-Asians. There has also been talk of a curse on the Lee family, an echo of which is reflected in the accidental death of Lee's

son, Brandon, during the filming of *The Crow*, when he was shot with what was meant to be a blank bullet but inexplicably turned out to be real.

Bruce Lee's life is colorfully explored in the 1993 film *Dragon*, which traces his rise to fame, showcases his awesome martial skills, and portrays some of the prejudice and racism he faced in this country. Now, years after his death, Lee remains a key figure in modern martial arts history, and the legacy of his teachings carries on with his students and in the art of *jeet kune do*.

JANET GEE AND CHOY LI FUT

More than twenty years ago, Janet Gee began studying the Chinese art of Choy Li Fut with Grandmaster Doc Fai Wong in San Francisco's Chinatown. Since that time, she has traveled all over the world teaching martial arts, has successfully competed in many tournaments, and has appeared on TV and in movies.

Developed in southern China in the 1830s by Chan Yeung, the Choy Li Fut system uses long-range fighting techniques, fast footwork, and flowing circular movements. Already a trained martial artist, Chan Yeung sought out a Shaolin master named Choy Fok for further study. Choy Fok lived on a mountainside and practiced Buddhism in silence. When Chan Yeung asked for lessons, Choy Fok told him he would teach only Buddhism, not the fighting arts.

Chan Yeung agreed to become Choy Fok's student on this spiritual path. But he still hoped to learn the secrets of the Shaolin masters that only Choy Fok could teach. So Chan Yeung studied Buddhism by day and practiced martial arts by himself late at night and in the early mornings.

One day Choy Fok interrupted Chan's practice. To test his skills, the old monk asked Chan to kick an eighty-pound boulder. Chan kicked the stone, and it traveled barely twelve feet. Unimpressed, the old monk put his foot to the rock and with a simple move sent it flying far into the air! It landed so far away that it was almost out of sight.

Chan Yeung studied with the monk for eight years and then returned to his village, where he developed his own style. He named his new system Choy Li Fut: *Choy* is in honor of the old monk, *Li* is after his first teacher, and *Fut* is a Chinese name for the Buddha.

"For me, martial arts is a way of life," Janet Gee says. "Not only has it enhanced my sense of well-being and my ability to defend myself in threatening situations; it has also given me a deeper purpose in life. Martial arts have been the way for me to understand inner peace."

CHINESE POWER
T'ai Chi, Hsing-I, and Pakua

The Chinese martial arts t'ai chi ch'uan, *hsing-i*, and *pakua* are sometimes referred to as "soft arts." Soft arts use more circular, internal, fluid movements to create power, whereas hard styles rely more on force and strength. Yet the terms are deceptive, since every art blends both soft and hard movements. Like the yin and the yang, each contains the other. The fluid movements of the soft arts are incredibly powerful, while breath and focus bring internal power to even the most physical of the hard arts.

These three Chinese arts use internal energy emanating from the *tan-tien* (the center of the body, slightly below the belly button) combined with external strength. In developing internal strength, practitioners learn about their opponents' energy in the practice of "push hands" and "sticky hands." In these exercises, two people engage in a subtle, yet powerful, play of arm and elbow movements, always with the limbs touching. Each anticipates the other's moves while attempting to find an opening in the opponent's energy. Both bodies twist and shift position in these highly skilled sparring exercises: A push hands master will use subtle shifts of energy and weight to beat his or her opponent.

Of these arts, t'ai chi ch'uan is the most well known. Although an accomplished t'ai chi master is a tough opponent, the fighting applications of this art are sometimes difficult to see. More easily recognized are the peace of mind and calmness of a t'ai chi practitioner.

T'ai chi students must be aware of each movement and every breath. Many people find this slow-moving art extremely difficult, preferring the faster, less meditative arts. Diligent t'ai chi training includes stance training, energy work, and the focus on each movement's fighting application. Forms, or set routines of movements, are both long and short, as there are various styles of t'ai chi. The forms work on developing *chi* and balancing the body's energy as well as perfecting a flow of movement. Many movements have beautiful names that correspond to elements of the natural world. "Cloud Hands" and "Grasp the Bird's Tail" are two such poetic postures.

Hsing-i ch'uan means "form of mind" or "body-mind boxing." This beautiful art follows the fighting movements of twelve animals: the dragon, tiger, horse, monkey, cock, turtle, hawk, swallow, snake, falcon, eagle, and bear. As in t'ai chi, *hsing-i* postures also work to enhance the flow of *chi* in the body. *Hsing-i* training is vigorous; the student develops strong internal power and is soon in excellent shape. The *hsing-i* student aims to leap like a tiger as well as move with the grace of a swallow. To cultivate quickness, practice

drills sometimes include tapping a hot iron.

The circular movements of the art of *pakua* trace patterns written in the classic Chinese philosophical text the *I Ching*, or Book of Changes. *Pakua* training begins with walking a circle, then changing direction and circling back. This movement is eventually paired with hand postures. Although *pakua* sounds boring, the dedication, awareness, and mindfulness of a *pakua* practitioner make the simple act of walking a beautiful martial dance. *Pakua* fighters are extremely skillful, full of surprises.

Many consider masters of these so-called soft arts to be the most daunting opponents of all. One true story tells of a famous t'ai chi master who was challenged by a group of zealous and skilled aikido teachers. The master invited the strongest and highest-ranking teacher to put him in the most difficult hold possible. With his arm twisted into a dangerous shoulder lock, the t'ai chi master simply placed his hand on the shoulder of the aikido teacher. The energy of the t'ai chi master sent the man slowly crumbling to the ground. The powers of a t'ai chi, *hsing-i*, or *pakua* master are difficult to match.

T'ai Chi and the Twisted Snake

Chang San-feng, a tall, bearded Taoist priest, is credited with developing the art of t'ai chi ch'uan. He was a well-known magistrate who gave up his respected position to study at the Shaolin Temple. After accomplishing mastery of the Shaolin arts, he retreated to a distant mountain range, searching to deepen his spiritual path and his self-defense practice.

One day, busy in his hut, he heard unusual noises outside. He looked out to see a coiled snake hissing at a hawk swooping in from atop a pine tree. The hawk anticipated a dinner of fresh snake, yet when it dove, the sinewy reptile twisted out of its way. The bird then tried to attack with its sharp talons, but the snake curled and circled, again evading the attack. The angry bird pecked and dove and tried to snatch the snake with its deadly claws. Still the snake managed to slither out of range.

After one attack, the snake wrapped itself around the bird's leg and from this position evaded the hawk's every attempt to peck its head. Finally, the hawk became weary. The snake took this prime opportunity to strike at the hawk's head with one direct, whiplike move. The bird died instantly.

Chang San-feng saw that a weaker creature could triumph over a stronger attacker if the weaker one was skilled in evasion. Through yielding, the snake was able to outperform the powerful hawk. Chang combined these observations with his study of nature—water, wind, and clouds—and his knowledge of Shaolin martial arts into the art of t'ai chi. He stressed the importance of flowing movements, the principles of yin and yang, and the stretching and contracting of muscles. Chang sought to create an art that focused on health and immortality rather than fighting and self-defense. Chang claimed that through the breath, the chi of the natural world could be channeled to blend with the infinite power of the universe.

WEN MEI YU

Born in China in 1936, Wen Mei Yu is a world-class t'ai chi teacher who moved to America to spread the healing nature of her art.

As a girl, Wen Mei Yu enjoyed sports such as basketball and Ping-Pong. She also studied acting, as well as both classical and traditional dance. Life went along smoothly until, at age seventeen, Wen Mei Yu fell sick with a bleeding ulcer. She was unable to eat the most simple foods, and neither eastern nor western medicines helped. It was suggested that she try *chi kung*, the traditional Chinese meditative practice and healing art.

In just a short time, Wen Mei Yu was able to eat again. As her health improved, she began training in several internal arts. For the last forty years, she has studied many forms and taught all over the world, promoting the health benefits of both t'ai chi and *chi kung*, among other martial arts.

"Children and adults who have trouble sitting still or find it hard to relax can be helped with t'ai chi or *chi kung* practice. The benefits are many, including greater confidence, a better ability to cope with stress, and sharper focus," she says. "The key is practice. When you practice regularly, you will discover what is right for you. You will also develop discipline, which is the greatest gift you can give yourself."

VALERIE LEE

Growing up in San Francisco's Chinatown in the 1970s, Valerie Lee had some familiarity with violence. Street fights often broke out in her neighborhood. Yet she was surprised when, at age thirteen, she was beaten up on the playground by three girls from a rival school. Val thinks they attacked her because of her status as a star school athlete, but she didn't have time to ask anything before they started hitting. When the dust settled, she was left with two black eyes and black-and-blue spots dotting her head and body. Her face was swollen and distorted.

Val's protective brother signed her up for karate classes. "He thought I should be able to fight," she says. "I needed to!"

"I never tell that story," Valerie now admits. "I don't want to give those bullies credit for my entry into martial arts. My brother is the one who deserves the credit." Yet, twenty-five years later, Valerie is thankful for her roundabout entry into martial arts training. Besides, several years after starting to train, Valerie got into another fight with the girls who had jumped her. This time, she was able to successfully defend herself. "I wasn't a very verbal kid," she says. "I tried to walk away but it didn't work."

For the next ten years, Valerie studied kung fu diligently, traveling to Asia on two occasions to compete in international tournaments. In Singapore, during her first world-class match, Val found herself up against a very strong opponent. "My teacher told me never to fight power against power," she says. "So when this opponent came at me, I circled the ring." Val lost this event, but she learned a lot. "I saw what happened when people did not hold back in a fight. People hit full force, not like we did in practice."

In her next title match, Val was victorious. She set her stance and threw her technique with just the right timing. "My opponent ran right into my punch," she says. "And it was a knockout!"

Val spent several years studying various styles, including a year at a Taoist monastery in Hawaii. Then a shoulder injury forced her to try something a little easier on her body. In 1981, she discovered Sifu Adam Hsu, teaching traditional northern-style Chinese kung fu in San Francisco's Golden Gate Park. Sifu Hsu had come from a long line of renowned masters and was himself well known. She started classes the next day and has been training ever since. Now an acupuncturist, Val travels around the world teaching these powerful arts.

"I was a good kid, and yet I was vulnerable to violence," she reflects. "And I needed to know how to protect myself. If I had been trained, I may have been able to reason with those girls, but no one had ever taught me."

A champion fighter herself, Val is also concerned with the sparring she sees at tournaments. "I see a lot of kicking and punching, but not much skill," she says. "Blocking and countering is more difficult but not given acknowledgment in tournaments. Often the less skilled, out-of-control fighter wins." She would like to see the tournament system change so that true martial skill is reflected in the match.

THE FATHER OF KARATE

In all things, one must have a clear mind.
— Gichin Funakoshi

Okinawa, a slim island grouping south of the main islands of Japan, is considered the birthplace of karate. Over the centuries, Okinawa was an obvious landing spot for travelers and explorers from both Japan and China. So perhaps Chinese priests or Japanese samurai brought the martial arts to these islands.

Having been under Chinese influence for many centuries, in 1609, Okinawa was conquered by the Satsuma clan of Japan. Under Japanese rule, the practice of martial arts was outlawed. Japanese soldiers swept the country, taking all traditional weapons such as knives and swords; possession of weapons could mean harsh punishment. However, many Okinawans had already developed strong fighting skills with their hands and feet and were able to band together against the invaders.

The art the Okinawans practiced was called *te*, the word for hand, and was practiced in the highest secrecy. Because the Okinawans needed to fight an enemy armed with weapons, the art of *te* had to be effective, powerful, and violent. Since no written records were kept, little is known about the development of *te* until the early 1900s, when the occupation of Okinawa relaxed to a degree.

Gichin Funakoshi, an Okinawan schoolteacher, is credited with having created the name *karate*. Born in 1868, Funakoshi was a sickly, shy boy with no confidence. To improve his health, he began to study martial arts with Master Azato, the father of one of his school friends. Master Azato taught his students under the cover of night. The students trained hard and scurried home before the sun came up. Funakoshi was a quick learner, and soon his health and confidence were blossoming.

When he was older, he became a schoolteacher. He taught his students martial arts exercises to keep them fit and strong. Officials noticed that his students stood out from the others, and it was discovered that their strength and health was due to his training. Although teaching martial arts was still outlawed, he was allowed to continue, and several years later the martial arts were finally made legal. By this time, Funakoshi had attracted hundreds of students.

Although he was often challenged, Funakoshi never once fought. Instead of accepting challenges from other people, he challenged himself. He practiced constantly. In the middle of huge windstorms, Funakoshi could be found outside, working on strengthening his stances.

The ruling prince of Japan invited Funakoshi to bring his martial arts to Tokyo. People were amazed by his demonstration of power and balance, and Funakoshi was swamped with requests to start classes. Living in a college dorm room with little money, he traded karate lessons for food. He lived simply, never smoked or drank alcohol, practiced every day, and wrote poetry. His free time was spent writing books about the philosophy and techniques of his art. Fourteen years later, in 1936, a group of Funakoshi's students built him a training hall.

Funakoshi wrote poetry under the name Shoto, which means the "swaying of the pine tree in the wind." Therefore his school was named Shotokan, and his style was called Shotokan karate.

The Americans who occupied Japan after World War II were impressed by Funakoshi's teaching. Many took classes from the legendary teacher, and he was invited to visit the United States. Eventually so many people wanted to learn his style that he sent his best students abroad to open their own schools. Shotokan is now particularly popular in the United States, and is practiced around the world as well.

KARATE

一

Karate as we know it now has branched into dozens of different arts, all stemming back to its Okinawan heritage. In general, karate styles focus on kicking and striking rather than wrestling or grappling. Shotokan, Shuri-ryu, Wado-ryu, Uechi-ryu, and Goju-ryu are some of the most popular of these arts. *Ryu* means formal school or style. Each art has different *kata*, or movement routines, and different techniques. For instance, Uechi-ryu emphasizes linear movements and dynamic *sanchin*, or belly, breathing. Tae kwon do and *hapkido* are Korean karate styles. Shaolin *kenpo* karate is an American style, and *cuong nu* originates in Vietnam.

Empty Hand

Until the early 1900s, the Chinese characters for "China hand" were used to represent the martial arts. *Kara* means Chinese, and *te* means hand. Okinawan master Gichin Funakoshi noticed that the symbol for "Chinese" looked similar to the symbol for "empty." He changed the symbol to read "empty hand," because he wanted his art to have a separate name from Chinese kung fu. The word *karate* means "the way of the empty hand."

空手

The First American Masters

In the 1800s, many Chinese immigrated to the United States to work building the transcontinental railroad. Others came drawn by the Californian gold rush. Although they brought their martial arts with them, they rarely shared them with non-Chinese people.

Hawaii was a stopping-off point for many Asian immigrants, and a few martial arts were introduced to the islands in the 1930s. As the arts spread, students of various styles began to compete against each other for dominance. In order to stop this fighting between styles, a group of top masters in Japanese, Chinese, and Okinawan arts cooperated to create the American art of *kajukenbo*. This powerful street fighting art is currently popular on the West Coast.

In addition to the influx of arts through Hawaii, after World War II and the Korean War, many American soldiers came back to this country excited about the martial arts they had learned while stationed overseas. Impressed by the skills of their Asian teachers, they were eager to spread the eastern arts to the west. These students opened some of the first American martial arts schools. Robert Trias, a military policeman and boxer, had studied kung fu while in the Navy. He saw that martial artists were more skilled in hand-to-hand combat than were western-style boxers. Trias studied in Okinawa, China, and Hawaii before returning to the United States mainland in 1946 to open one of the first karate schools run by a westerner, in Phoenix, Arizona. Trias also organized a professional karate association and hosted the first official American karate competition in 1955.

Nunchaku and Other Okinawan Farm Tools

Under Japanese rule, the Okinawan people were stripped of all weapons. Yet the Japanese let the Okinawan farmers keep their farm tools, a decision they would later regret. The clever Okinawans turned the rough tools into fearsome weapons.

Nunchaku, traditionally used for harvesting rice, are two short, hard wood sticks connected by a small rope. *Nunchaku* can be twirled at great speeds. The hard ends of the wooden poles are deadly. When spun, they can be used to block other weapons or strike from a safe distance. *Nunchaku* can also be used to pull a weapon out the hands of an opponent or trap an attacker in a choke. Beginners practice with rubber *nunchaku*. The wooden sticks are far too dangerous both to the student and those nearby!

The *tonfa* is actually the handle of a rice grinder. A long stick with a handle on one end, it can protect the forearm from attack or block other weapons. It can also be spun and thrust as an offensive weapon.

Demonstrations at modern martial arts tournaments often show these ancient farm tools. It is fascinating to think that the Okinawans developed these weapons only because their true weapons were taken away.

A steel tool with three prongs, the *sai* was used to plant seeds. As a weapon, however, the Okinawan peasants used this tool to block attacking swords, as well as to stab and slash. *Sai* are usually worked in pairs, with one for blocking and one for attacking.

JUJUTSU AND
JUDO
—

Both judo and jujutsu have their origins in *chin na*, a wrestling and grappling art that evolved in the 1600s and is rarely practiced outside of China today. *Chin* means to capture, and *na* means to hold. *Chin na* moves are geared toward restraining and holding an opponent and were historically used by soldiers and police officers against criminals. Each *chin na* move is rooted in medical knowledge of the body. The study of bones, muscles, and vital organs is a big part of *chin na* practice. Knowing whether muscles will tear or stretch and whether bones will snap or bend teaches one how to manipulate the body.

Ancient *chin na* moves are found in the modern art of jujutsu, a Japanese art of self-defense. The word *jujutsu* means "art of flexibility." The art encompasses throwing, locking joints, choke holds, defending against weapons, and striking with speed and accuracy. Advanced jujutsu students strike specific targets on the body in order to immobilize, disable, or stun an attacker. Deadly jujutsu strikes are called *atemi*.

Unlike other arts, jujutsu has no central founder. In the nineteenth century, when the art was popular in Japan, there were many schools, each with its own variations of throwing and locking techniques. Some teachers combined jujutsu with techniques from other arts such as aikido and various karate styles. Some schools taught weapons; others did not. Because there is no centralized organization, modern jujutsu styles are varied and diverse.

Many people interested in self-defense study jujutsu because it is so practical. A jujutsu student will learn to escape from common attacks such as being grabbed from behind, pulled by the arm, or punched. Jujutsu must be practiced carefully because the joint locking techniques are dangerous. Students are taught to "slap out" during practice to show that they have been effectively immobilized by such a hold. Once the student slaps the mat with his or her free hand, the opponent will release him or her.

Judo, which means "gentle way," is more of an art or sport than a system of fighting or self-defense. In the late 1800s, the founder of judo, Dr. Jigaro Kano, took the kicks, punches, and dangerous locking and breaking moves out of the art of jujutsu in order to create judo. An educator, Kano sought to create an art that developed the connection between mind and body. He formulated moves that were practiced in pairs, with one person allowing the other to perform the technique. He also believed strongly in respect for tradition and put forward a spirit of cooperation rather than competition in his art. Kano opened his Kodokan judo training center in Tokyo in 1882.

Kano likened good judo to a willow tree. When heavy snow lands on the branch of a firm oak tree, even the strongest branch eventually breaks. But when snow piles onto the branch of a willow tree, the flexible branch will bend, spilling the snow onto the ground. The branch will spring right back. Judo principles teach never to meet force with force.

Today judo has evolved into a much more competitive art than Kano envisioned. Judo was one of the first martial arts to come to the United States, and since 1972 it has been an Olympic sport. Players compete in several weight classes with the goal of throwing their opponents off balance. Arm bars, hold-downs, and pins are used to control one's opponent. To end the match, the contestants try to score an *ippon*. An *ippon* is won either by pinning an opponent for thirty seconds or by locking him or her in a deadly arm bar. An *ippon* is also scored by throwing an opponent onto his or her back.

Points are awarded depending on the form of the technique. A good, clean throw, lock, or choke earns a whole point. Half a point is given if the technique is merely passable. If no *ippon* is scored, the winner is determined after a five-minute round for men or a four-minute round for women.

Traditionally judo was practiced on tatami, mats made of rice straw. Today judo mats are made of plastic and foam.

LILIKO OGASAWARA

At three years old, Liliko Ogasawara was the best student in her father's judo class. Even so, she waited until she was four years old to start competing.

At twenty-three, Ogasawara is now ranked the number-one female in her division in the United States and third in the world. To compete in judo tournaments, she has traveled from her home in California to many countries, including Japan, Spain, Germany, England, Australia, France, and Poland. "In every country I have broadened my horizons," she says. "It was really interesting to see other cultures and hear different languages. It was also scary to fight all those kids from other places, but it was worth it to be able to travel."

Growing up, Ogasawara spent every afternoon after school at the *dojo*. She watched several classes in addition to participating in at least two. Weekends were spent traveling to tournaments. On Mondays, she usually brought trophies in for show-and-tell.

"Occasionally other kids gave me a hard time," she says. "They wanted to fight me. My dad told me to tell them to come to the *dojo* and I would be happy to fight them there." Not surprisingly, no one ever accepted her challenge.

Being serious about training had drawbacks. Ogasawara sometimes felt that she missed out on having a normal social life like her schoolmates. It was also difficult to "make weight" before tournaments. "I was growing like any normal person, but I always had to lose weight to compete in my division," she says. "I hated starving myself and dieting. I started get a complex about my weight." Eventually she decided to let her body find its natural weight. Now she doesn't diet, and she strongly encourages other kids to accept whatever size body they have.

After the 1996 Olympics, Ogasawara plans to retire from judo and look for a job in television. She will continue to practice, but only for fun.

Of the last twenty years of training she says, "Doing a positive thing like judo helped me to develop physical and mental discipline, and practicing kept me out of trouble. The hard work was definitely worth it."

AIKIDO

—

True victory is not defeating an enemy. True victory gives love and changes the enemy's heart.
— Morihei Ueshiba, founder of aikido

The founder of aikido, Morihei Ueshiba, was a spiritual person. As a young man in the early 1900s, he studied swordsmanship and jujutsu and was a skilled bayonet fighter. His teacher, an old-style samurai, was a legendary fighter. Many people sought him out as a teacher, and he instructed both the police and the military.

But Ueshiba knew that even though his teacher was feared by others, he was always afraid of his enemies. The teacher never went out without his weapons, and he slept with a pair of sharpened chopsticks by his side. Ueshiba prepared and tasted the master's food because the teacher believed it might be poisoned.

Ueshiba pondered his teacher's fear. He saw that his teacher trained extremely hard, was in top form, and had amazing skill. But he seemed to fear that someday someone would train harder, be in better shape, and have more skill. Ueshiba came to realize that the goal of being better than everyone else had serious limitations. This was the source of his teacher's worries. There could always be a better fighter out there, and thinking that one always had to be the best was potentially dangerous. Ultimately Ueshiba came to believe that victory through violence could lead only to more violence.

In the early 1920s, he had an experience that taught him another important lesson. His father fell sick, and so Ueshiba set off to pay him a visit. While traveling, he visited a new spiritual teacher, Onisaburo Deguchi, who encouraged Ueshiba to become his bodyguard and teach his followers martial arts. Deguchi's religion, which sought to bring together people from different races and religions, appealed to Ueshiba, so he accepted the offer.

One day the group was ambushed by hostile soldiers carrying guns. Ueshiba prepared to die but suddenly found himself flooded with a strange energy. Concentrating even in the middle of crossfire, Ueshiba saw the bullets like "pebbles of white light" as they flew through the air. Twisting and turning his body with grace and speed, he eluded every bullet.

After this experience, Ueshiba retreated to the mountains to meditate under a sacred waterfall. Ueshiba understood that the calmer he became, the more clearly he could see the violent thoughts and actions of other people.

In 1925, when Ueshiba was forty-two years old, a teacher of swordsmanship came to study with him. But an argument ensued, and the man struck at Ueshiba with a wooden sword. Ueshiba dodged every strike. The man retreated in awe.

Later that same morning, while walking in the garden, Ueshiba felt a flash of extreme lightness. "I was able to understand the whisperings of the birds, and was clearly aware of the mind of God," he wrote in his autobiography. Ueshiba believed he finally understood the heart of the martial arts: "God's love — the spirit of loving protection for all beings." Ueshiba cried tears of joy.

Morihei Ueshiba's spiritual awakening led him to develop a new martial art, which he named aikido. Ai means harmony, and ki is the Japanese word for chi, the vital energy found in every breath, and throughout the universe. The goal of aikido is to harmonize this life force in the individual with that at work in the world.

Aikido looks like a circular dance, with lots of spinning and graceful takedowns. The aikido student leads the oncoming energy of the opponent into a throw, finishing with a joint lock or wrist twist, blending his or her energy with that of the opponent and defeating the opponent by his or her own violence.

Aikido students wear either traditional judo uniforms or judo jackets and black split skirts called *hakama*. Training starts with learning to fall properly, followed by throwing, and moving in circular patterns. Aikido is performed both standing and kneeling.

Some aikido schools train with short wooden staffs or spears. Advanced students learn to deal with groups of attackers, a skill for which Ueshiba was famous. Awareness of distance, timing, and the intentions of the enemy are important factors in aikido training.

Aikido training is done with a partner: The *uke* attacks, and the *nage* defends. Students practice as both *uke* and *nage* to experience the feelings on both sides of the confrontation. When both partners pay attention and respect each other's skill, aikido looks smooth and flowing. But when one person loses attention or shows off, injuries may occur.

While in his seventies, Ueshiba was filmed defending himself nearly effortlessly against five or six men. "I cannot be defeated," he said. "I am victorious right from the start. As soon as the thought of attack crosses my opponent's mind, he shatters the harmony of the universe and is instantly defeated regardless of how quickly he attacks."

KENDO AND IAIDO

The sword, the mind, and the body are one.
— samurai saying

Kendo is the Japanese art of fencing. Though once a means of survival, the art is no longer geared toward combat. Matches are scored, and sticks must hit specific targets on the body in order to earn points. In addition, the name of the target must be called out as it is hit. Matches are colorful events with lots of yelling. Kendo is a highly ritualized art, and the student must work at achieving a clear mind and a strong spirit while executing perfect technique and correct posture.

The kendo student looks like a relative of the old samurai. The basic uniform is a heavy cotton jacket paired with a *hakama*, or traditional split skirt. In addition, a helmet with metal grills protects the face and shoulders, a breastplate acts as body armor, and padded gloves cover the hands and wrists. Swords, called *shinai*, are made from sticks of bamboo strapped with leather.

In the art of *iaido*, students use real swords. The *iaido* practitioner must draw the sword from its sheath, wield it, and replace it with a steady hand. Balance is essential in this art, as is concentration. A slip in focus may mean the loss of a finger. A swift draw is also important, as a student who unsheathes his or her sword slowly is likely to be attacked before the blade is out.

Iaido developed from classic sword training for combat, when old masters of the fighting arts saw that military students could develop character through an intensely focused practice. Each *iaido* form consists of four moves: *nukitsuke,* drawing the sword from the sheath; *kiritsuke,* cutting with the blade; *chiburi,* shaking the blood from the blade; and *noto,* returning the sword to its sheath. Beginning students use blunt swords, while advanced practitioners work with sharp blades. The sharp blades can be lethal, though, and extreme respect is shown to the swords at all times. *Iaido* students are usually formal and serious people who enjoy an art that demands precision and perfection.

Do and Budo

Do means "way" or "path." When added to the name of a Japanese martial art, it shows that the style is more than a military or combat system. It indicates that the art has a spiritual component and is geared toward character development. *Kendo,* aikido, *iaido,* and judo have incorporated this philosophy into their training.

Budo means "way of fighting" and is an overall term for the spiritually oriented martial arts of Japan. *Budo* refers to the mind of the warrior who strives to overcome ego and self-consciousness and work toward harmony and peace.

The Japanese Sword

The Japanese swordsmith heats a block of ore, a specific hard metal found in a particular mine, and hammers it flat. He then splits it in half with a chisel and folds the two halves together. He repeats this process many times over several months. Each time the metal is folded together and layered, it becomes stronger. When the blade is finished, the swordsmith sharpens it in a delicate process, by heating it, then dipping it in cool liquid. The skilled swordsmith is able to regulate the exact temperature of the blade by looking at the color of the hot metal. The sharpening process gives the blade a deadly slicing edge, while keeping it soft enough inside so that it has flexibility. The swordsmith then polishes the blade by hand, rubbing it over a series of limestones until it shines like a mirror.

Students of Japanese sword arts learn the proper care and respect for their weapons. Even oil and dirt from fingerprints will leave ugly marks on a finely honed blade. Breathing on the sword is also avoided, as it may leave moisture on the blade. People serious about taking care of their sword follow a specific method and ritual for cleaning these traditionally honored weapons.

In the time of the samurai, the sword was considered the soul of the warrior. Not only did it show his ability to cut down an opponent, but the sword was also a symbol of how the humble samurai had cut down his own ego.

THE NINJA

—

Ninja were introduced to America through movies and television. Most everybody knows of the comical *Teenage Mutant Ninja Turtles.* Yet *ninjutsu,* the art of being invisible, has been around for a long time. Between the eleventh and sixteenth centuries, the ninja acted as secret agents for the samurai.

The samurai fought on horseback and thought spying dishonorable, so they hired ninja to do their clandestine work. Living in the forests, men, women, and children alike worked as loyal ninja to their samurai clan. Female ninja were called "deadly flowers."

The fighting arts of the ninja were kept hidden. To learn *ninjutsu,* one had to be born into a family of ninja. The training was hard and started at a young age. Ninja had to run, jump, and climb with speed and ease. They learned to escape from being tied with ropes and to leap quietly from tree to tree. Using a tiny bamboo reed to breathe, the ninja trained to stay underwater for many hours. They could also go without food or sleep for many days. Young ninja learned to walk through water like the crane, move through tight spots like a sand crab, and slink across mats like an octopus.

Traveling under the cover of night, the ninja dressed from head to toe in dark colors. During the day, they wore disguises or costumes, often changing clothes several times. A ninja might pretend to be a poor beggar to get close to an enemy. A woman might present herself as a dancer or servant in order to gain entry to an enemy's home. This "deadly flower" might be carrying a hidden weapon such as a poison-tipped fan.

The ninja were skilled with many weapons, but their signature weapon was the *shuriken*, or throwing star. An iron disc with five spikes, the *shuriken* does not kill but causes an enemy to back up or run away to avoid being cut. An accomplished ninja could accurately throw a *shuriken* from a distance of up to thirty feet.

The ninja used just about anything they could find in combat. They flung nets over their enemies and dropped small spiked balls to pierce the feet of oncoming attackers. They mixed poisonous plants into food, and slipped powders that caused sneezing, itching, and worse into the homes of enemies. In tight spaces, ninja set small bombs to give them a chance to "vanish into thin air." They climbed walls with the help of spiked bands strapped to their hands and feet. Amazing climbers, ninja were called "human flies" or "spiders of the night." They used capes to "fly"

off ledges, springboards to jump over fences, and even attached themselves to kites to swoop over enemy walls. Secret passageways, trapdoors, and tunnels were all part of the ninja's underground world.

It was rumored that ninja were shape changers who could turn into animals or objects if they were pursued. This too was a secret trick. A ninja might carry a monkey dressed in exactly the same clothing as himself. If the ninja was chased into the woods or was cornered, he or she would let the monkey go. This "transformation" would frighten the attackers, and they would abandon the chase. The ninja could then sneak to safety. A ninja also might roll into a tight ball and pretend to be a rock, or if caught in the middle of a field, act like a scarecrow.

The ninja communicated with each other by music, whistles, and smoke signals. A certain tune could mean attack or retreat. Special mirrors were kept hidden in the woods so signals could be flashed across great distances.

Though they were masters of deception, the ninja believed in the yin-yang balance of life. They studied nature for inspiration and guidance. When peace finally came to Japan, some ninja went to work for the secret police. Over a period of several hundred years, the art of *ninjutsu* began to die out. Despite the popularity of ninja in movies and on television, today there are only a few masters left who teach the true ninja skills.

A MODERN NINJA

Stephen K. Hayes is a Buddhist priest as well as a *shidoshi*, a "teacher of the warrior way of enlightenment," the art of *ninjutsu*. Having earned his black belt in karate by the age of twenty-five, Hayes read about the art of the ninja and was driven to find a way to study this secret art. Blindly he bought a ticket to Japan. Luck and coincidence brought him to an accomplished teacher, and he has now been training for twenty-nine years.

"Real ninja are protectors," he says. "And they are heroes. Unfortunately the ninja we are shown in the movies are not always real heroes. Do they care about other people? Do they care about their communities? Do they want people to have a good experience in life? This is what true protectors and heroes are working for."

The kids in Hayes's classes at the Nine Gates Institute in Dayton, Ohio, start by making a commitment to themselves, their school, and their teachers. They also must agree to "protect their homes" by making contributions such as taking out the trash or feeding the family pets.

"The ninja were not praised in public," Hayes explains. "They worked in the shadows. It is the same today. We do nice things for other people without them having to thank us, sometimes even without them knowing."

Concentration is necessary for ninja training, as is confidence. Every ninja learns how to protect himself or herself, such as by tucking and rolling with a punch or escaping swiftly from another student's grip. Basic training begins with evading strikes from huge foam bats that are swung like swords.

After three decades of training, Shidoshi Hayes is still learning. "There will come a time when every one of us will doubt ourselves and think about quitting. Those are the times when it is necessary to remake our vows. You may commit to keep training, go for the next rank, or decide you want to get your black belt. Later, remembering what you did to keep going, you are most proud of your training," he says. "Everyone thinks he or she is the only one who goes through this questioning. All of us, even the champions, go through times of doubting. Be strong of spirit. Keep going!"

The Ninja's Chinese Counterparts

The *lin kuei*, "forest demons," are the ninja's Chinese cousins. Living in the forests, they were thought to have mystical powers, though most of their fabled abilities are not much different from those taught in other martial arts. They were adept at tracking and could imitate the sounds of wild animals in order to scare their enemies. They were able to live off the land and concoct poisons from plants and were also said to escape from being bound up with ropes by dislocating their joints.

CAPOEIRA

—

Few people think of Brazil as a center of martial training. But as far back as the sixteenth century, *capoeira* was being practiced by African slaves working in Brazilian farmlands.

Brazilian slave owners forbade any kind of martial practice, so the African slaves practiced an art that looked like an innocent dance. The slave owners saw a colorful game; accompanied by music and song, the kicks, sweeps, and leg locks of the *capoeiristas* looked like circus movements. Yet the Africans were actually training hard. Developed from *atombe*, an African fighting system, the fight-dance hid lethal techniques.

In an environment where punishment often meant the loss of an arm, the *capoeiristas* focused their art on kicks and headstands. Even if their arms were chained behind their backs, they could still practice.

Over time, *capoeira* grew popular in the cities and countryside and was practiced in the streets by the poorer population. It was made illegal by Brazilian lawmakers who were threatened by the idea of people learning to defend themselves, and around 1900, the police set out to destroy all *capoeira* centers in the African-Brazilian communities. Still, due to the dedication of several powerful masters, the art survived.

In the 1930s, an elderly master from the province of Bahia, Mestre (Master) Bimba, finally convinced the lawmakers that *capoeira* was a cultural art form. Although many people still disapproved of the practice, in 1932, Mestre Bimba opened the first legal training school. Even now, however, there is prejudice against *capoeiristas* in some parts of Brazil.

Today *capoeira* is practiced all over the world as a sport, an art, and a way to keep in shape. Taught mainly by Brazilians, the *capoeira* tradition acknowledges the suffering of the slaves who developed the art. Its influence can be seen in many dance styles, including in the head spinning movements of American break dancing.

Capoeira is highly acrobatic and theatrical. The players smile while turning cartwheels, performing headstands, and dancing. *Capoeira* is always accompanied by music, and students learn to play instruments and sing as part of their training. The lead instrument in the *capoeira* circle is the *berimbau*, which originated in Africa and is composed of a one-stringed wooden bow with a dried gourd attached. The other instruments are the *pandeiro*, or tambourine; the *atabaque*, a tall drum; and the *agogo*, made from two bells. The *berimbau* player starts the music, and the others follow the lead. The rhythm of the *berimbau* sets the pace of the fighters.

The *berimbau* player also sings the main song line, while the other musicians and players form a choir. Although the songs may sound simple, they often tell a different story from the one that is actually spoken. In this way, *capoeiristas* of the past were able to keep the art hidden from outsiders while at the same time passing the traditions on to the next generation.

PENTJAK SILAT

—

Indonesia is made up of three thousand islands and is home to nearly as many styles of *pentjak silat*, Indonesian martial arts. Most styles include fierce and practical self-defense techniques—gracefully accompanied by music and drumming.

In the hot climate of Indonesia, practice is often held in the cool of the night with the sound of the drums signaling the beginning of a training session. *Pentjak silat* is not practiced for sport, so there are few rules in the fighting. Indonesian martial artists attack with many different techniques: kicks, hand strikes, holds, and joint locks. All parts of the body are used as weapons, including the elbows, knees, knuckles, heels, and head. Rolling, high kicking, and striking from a crouched position mimic the movements of jungle animals, including the tiger, snake, monkey, and crane. Although Indonesian fighters can look wild, their fighting techniques are actually refined and specific. A good fighter will be intimidating to his or her opponent, with the eyes being particularly frightening.

Harimau is a *silat* style that follows the movements of the tiger. Developed in wet, slippery areas, where it was impossible to fight standing up, *harimau* movements require strong, flexible legs for staying low to the ground and leaping from all fours. Due to the uneven terrain of the Indonesian islands, most *pentjak silat* stylists are strong ground fighters. Training is done on rough, rocky ground, on marshland, and even in the sea.

Weapons such as the spear, the staff, the iron chain, and knives of many shapes are included in *pentjak silat* training. The kris, a wavy-bladed, double-edged knife reputed to have magic powers, is the most sacred of all Indonesian weapons. The blow pipe is used to shoot poisoned arrows. Short razors are gripped between the toes. Women use beautiful fans in *silat* forms that look like traditional dance. However, the metal points of the fans are sharpened and sometimes dipped in deadly herbs.

The master teacher of *pentjak silat* is called *pandekar* (sometimes spelled *pendekkar*), which means "professional" or "clever mind." A teacher may also be called *guru*. Indonesian teachers are healers and are sometimes reputed to be mind readers.

In many areas of Indonesia, training sessions are held in secret and at midnight, a time considered sacred. Indonesian martial arts place high regard on both the beauty of the movements and the spiritual powers of the fighter. During training, students of the Indonesian arts are encouraged to connect with their own spirit and the powers of the universe. Often, accomplished students will look as though they are in a trance, so completely immersed are they in the world of the animal spirits and in their own *ilmu*, the Indonesian equivalent of *chi*.

The Kris

The kris is a double-sided, wavy-bladed knife. The spirit of the kris is held to be so powerful that Indonesian martial artists handle these weapons with great care and respect. It is said that a kris might rattle when an enemy approaches or fly into the air to warn of danger.

Krisses range from less than ten to more than thirty inches long. The handle and sheath are beautifully decorated, and the wavy edge of the blade is believed to reflect the weapon's spirit. The kris maker hammers together many layers of molten metal to forge the blade. He then uses his bare hands to fashion the sharp edge, leaving his fingerprints in the hot metal. Respected for his talents and spiritual powers, the kris maker holds an honored position in the community.

A Mighty Shout

In the late 1960s, a frail, older Indonesian master demonstrated his spiritual powers for a group of visiting Japanese karate teachers. As a large rock was placed before the master, the Japanese experts shook their heads. They were certain the rock could not be broken with bare hands. The Indonesian master studied the rock for a long time. He took water and poured it over his hands, chanting quietly. He paused, then suddenly opened his mouth and let out a resounding shout. Although the master had never even touched the rock, it crumbled. Shocked, the Japanese masters bowed deeply with respect.

POEKOELAN

—

The thorn protects the rose and
hurts only those who would steal the blossom.
— old saying

Poekoelan tjiminde tulen is a beautiful martial art brought to the United States from Indonesia in 1956 by Guru Willy Wetzel. *Poekoelan* means a "series of strikes with hands and feet." *Tjiminde* means "beautiful flowing river," and *tulen* means "first" or "original."

The symbol of *poekoelan* is a red rose and two sticks of bamboo on a black background. A rose is beautiful to look at, but if you get too close, its thorns will scratch and hurt. In a strong wind, even a slim, weak-looking piece of bamboo is flexible; it might bend but will snap back fiercely. *Poekoelan* students are taught to be beautiful and deadly like the rose, and strong and flexible like the bamboo.

Poekoelan students study self-defense, Indonesian dance, and traditional drumming in order to learn the whole of this vast art. As in Indonesia, practice is often held at midnight, a time when the body's natural energy is believed to be strongest. *Poekoelan* is a strenuous art, with tests often lasting several days and including long periods of meditation. *Kumbongs* are the Indonesian equivalent of sets or *kata*. Each student creates her or his own *kumbong* from *jurus*, or striking combinations, and from the movements of the crane, tiger, monkey, and snake. When a student is performing a *kumbong*, her or his spirit should be apparent to the observer. A strong spirit reflects a true heart, the utmost goal of the *poekoelan* fighter.

BARBARA NIGGEL

Barbara Niggel started training with Willy Wetzel when she was twelve years old, more than thirty years ago. She is now the head of the *poekoelan* system. She remembers Wetzel as a kind, compassionate man, "the most loving man I have ever known."

Niggel trained every day for hours and hours, and spent most of her weekends with her teacher. Lessons were held at night, in the dark, in order to develop her eyesight. Hours spent striking X rays improved the speed of her hand techniques. Kicking a soccer ball against a wall increased the speed of her kicks. "Be like lightning!" Wetzel urged her. "It strikes fast, without warning and just as quickly, disappears!"

Guru Wetzel's teaching and Niggel's training paid off. While still in her teens, she became a world champion.

"*Poekoelan* is a broken-mirror style," say says. "If you throw a rock at a mirror, it breaks in many different directions. Each student of this art moves in a different way, a way that is right for them."

TAE KWON DO
—

Tae kwon do has its beginnings in a martial art called *t'aekyon*, which existed in Korea thirteen hundred years ago. Over the centuries, Koreans failed to develop strong iron-working skills, so their swords were inferior to those of their often unfriendly Chinese neighbors. They did develop effective weaponless fighting skills—*tae* means "to kick," and *kyon* or *kwon* means "to strike with the fist."

In the early 1900s, under Japanese rule, Koreans were forbidden to practice martial arts. The ban was lifted only during World War II, as martial arts study was part military training. After the war, when Korea won its independence, its leaders sought to increase national pride by encouraging the practice of traditional martial arts. In 1950, Choi Hong Hi, a Korean officer, began training his troops in ancient *t'aekyon*, and many Americans stationed in South Korea eagerly trained alongside his students. When these men returned to America, they brought with them their enthusiasm for this new art. Choi renamed the art tae kwon do, adding *do* to show that the art was meant to be a way of life, not just a method of combat.

Tae kwon do is the most practiced martial art in the United States, due in part to the visibility of Hollywood tae kwon do champion Chuck Norris. Jhoon Rhee, a Korean, also brought much attention to tae kwon do when he came to this country in 1957 to go to college. His flashy demonstrations of board breaking and skillful kicking techniques led him to teach tae kwon do to the American Secret Service and at other government agencies. Rhee's students now run schools in many states and in several foreign countries as well.

Tae kwon do is popular in more than 140 countries. A competitive style that emphasizes kicking techniques, tae kwon do will be an Olympic sport in the year 2000. In competition, students wear padded boots, gloves, headgear, and chest protectors. Advanced students execute high jumps and spinning kicks and are able to break boards, bricks, and tiles in midair.

Although some people criticize tae kwon do for its emphasis on kicking, a look at the terrain and history of Korea will help explain it. Horseback was a common mode of travel through Korea's expanses of open country. So high kicks, to topple an opponent from his horse, were effective opening maneuvers.

OTHER ARTS OF THE WORLD

—

After World War II, Burmese *bando* became known in the west. A kicking art, it also includes unusual choke holds and fast strikes. The black panther is the *bando* symbol, black suggesting the unknown the fighter faces every day.

Thai boxing, also called kick boxing, is popular in the United States and Europe. In this art, fast punches are followed by strong leg and knee strikes. Then, in close-range fighting, opponents lock body to body. Many Thai boxers are religious and pray before competition. Events with cash prizes are held in Thailand, the United States, and Europe. Savate is a French kick-boxing art.

Filipino stick fighting, called *escrima* or *arnis*, uses two short pieces of bamboo. Fighters twirl the light sticks in fast patterns that both block and strike. The first goal of a stick fighter is to disarm his or her opponent, as an unarmed fighter is less dangerous than one wielding a knife, stick, or broken bottle. Stick fighting is practical for self-defense. Few people carry around bamboo sticks, but an umbrella, a cane, or even a tree branch can be just as effective if used skillfully in a street attack. *Escrima* was once taught secretly only in the Philippines but is now practiced all over the world.

The art of *samo-aborona bez oruzhia*, which means "self-defense without a weapon," is practiced in areas of Russia. Known as *sambo*, matches are popular and are scored like judo competitions.

INDIA

Back to the Source

—

If instead of fighting with him you say to your enemy, "You have won" and bow before him, that is the biggest deed in the world.
— Mathavan Asan, master of the southern style of kalaripayit

Bodhidharma left India thousands of years ago, but the ancient ways of the traditional Indian warrior are still practiced today in the art of *kalaripayit*. *Kalari* means "battlefield," and *payit* means "practice."

Kalaripayit is a colorful art, full of ritual and religious customs. The students always pay respect to Garuda, the god of strength, and Hanuman, the monkey god. Kali, the goddess of war, is also honored. Some *kalaripayit* movements copy those of traditional Indian dances.

The *Kalaripayit* training room, decorated with flowers and leaves, contains a large castle made of sand. Called the *poothara*, the castle has six levels. The first five levels represent the senses: smell, touch, taste, sound, and sight. The highest level represents the sixth sense: intuition, the combination of thought and feeling. A chair and a pair of sandals are placed in front of the *poothara* to show respect for the long line of teachers who have carried the art through the centuries.

Kalari training is extremely demanding. Sessions can last up to sixteen hours. Before beginning, students oil their bodies, then wrap themselves with special clothes. The start of the session is marked by the sounding of a conch shell, blown like a horn. Students never eat before training, and a special soup is taken after the class.

Kalaripayit includes hand-to-hand combat, fighting with bamboo sticks, weapons training, and for the advanced students, the secret techniques of *marma-adi*. Marma-adi practice involves strikes to vital targets on the body. These blows can kill or stun a person without leaving any mark. Only very advanced and trusted students are taught these techniques. Because of the intensity of training, *kalari* teachers are also experienced doctors. Should a student be knocked out in training, they are able to revive him quickly.

Part Three

—

TRAINING TODAY

—

Expect everything from yourselves.
— Sakyamuni Buddha

Throughout history, people have flocked to training halls to learn the secrets of the famous fighting arts. But it has never been easy to study martial arts. Men and women who wished to become students at the Shaolin monastery waited for a long time to enroll. Showing up day after day, waiting at the temple gates, in rain, snow, or blazing sun, they had to prove their desire to train.

Once a dedicated few were taken as students, the real hard work started. The new students spent many months — sometimes even a year — doing chores for the teachers and the other students. They were required to carry water, sweep and scrub the training hall, gather herbs and medicines, and feed and attend to the teachers.

Only if the students performed all the chores and did not seem overeager to begin martial arts training were they finally allowed to start studying the simple techniques. Learning to wait made humble and patient students, and eventually humble and patient martial artists.

Today it is much easier to study the martial arts. In modern schools, new students may learn several simple techniques in their first few classes. But although the techniques may look easy, it takes years of practice to refine each movement and put spirit and force behind each move. In addition, most schools still require students to clean the training hall and help keep the school running smoothly. In some styles, teaching others is an important part of the training and a way to give back to the school.

The Dojo, Kwoon, or School

—

Japanese refer to a martial art school as a *dojo*, which means "place of the way." *Kwoon* is the Chinese word for training hall. In all arts, the schools are respected and kept clean and neat. Before class begins, it is customary for students to sweep the floors and polish the mirrors.

There are several titles for "teacher." At Japanese schools, the teacher is called *sensei*. *Sen* means "before," and *sei* means "born." Therefore the teacher is the "one who was born before." In Chinese arts, the teacher is called *sifu*. *Mestre* is the title of a *capoeira* master.

While students are learning from their teachers, the teachers are becoming better martial artists through instructing. In *poekoelan tjiminde tulen*, teacher and students mark the end of class by saying the Indonesian phrase "*Gotong-rayong*," which means that all who train do so in the spirit of working together. It might translate to something like "Share and share alike."

In every martial art, students honor and respect their teacher. A student might show this respect by bringing the teacher a cup of tea or by carrying his or her training bag. We who "come after" are able to study these wonderful arts because of each teacher's continuing commitment and generosity.

Nighttime Adventure

Many years ago at a Japanese monastery, a certain monk would jump over the mud wall every night to go into the town. There, he drank and chatted with the villagers.

The master knew about these secret escapades. One evening he sat in meditation at the exact spot where the monk came over the wall upon returning to the monastery. After carousing, the monk stumbled home. So drunk that he didn't even realize what was happening, he hopped over the wall and landed right on his master's head. But the next day, when he was told that the master was suffering from a horrible headache, he knew what he had done. The monk felt so badly about being disrespectful that he dedicated himself fully to his studies. Later in life, he became a great Zen master.

THE BOW

Students of the martial arts spend a lot of time bowing. A bow is a greeting, like shaking hands or saying hello. It is also a way to show respect. In most styles, students bow before walking on or off the training floor or mat, as a way to express respect for the place of learning.

Practitioners also bow at the beginning and end of every class, and to workout partners during class. The bow is a way of saying, "I respect you, and you respect me." Students always bow to their teacher, and if the teacher is not present, the bow is often made to a photograph.

There are as many types of bows as there are styles of martial arts. Aikido bows are made on one's knees. The bow of the American art *kajukenbo* is made with a closed fist covered by an open fist. The hands are pushed out from the waist to show that the skilled fist is guarded by the open hand, indicating that the student will respect his or her partner.

In *poekoelan*, a beginner bows by bending at the waist with both feet apart. An advanced bow, with the hands together in a prayer position, is earned after the first six months of training.

MEDITATION

—

In quietness and confidence will be your strength.
— Isaiah

Meditation is the foundation of the original martial artists. The monks of the Shaolin Temple spent many hours in meditation each day. By learning to clear their minds, they were better able to focus on the task at hand.

A period of meditation may begin each training session. Beginners often find it difficult to meditate and sit still. The mind is usually teaming with thoughts. Paying attention to the breath helps settle both the mind and the body. When the mind is full, it is difficult to learn. Meditating is also referred to as "emptying one's cup." In order to pour a fresh serving of tea, the cold, stale tea must first be emptied from the cup. In the same way, the student's expectations, worries, and jumbled thoughts must be cleared away in order to make room for what will be taught in class.

To focus during meditation, it is helpful to count. One may silently count "one" on the inhale and "two" on the exhale. If a thought flits in, one should just start over again from "one." Even for advanced students, it is sometimes hard to get past "one"!

In some arts, meditation is done in the *seiza* position, with the legs folded underneath and the body resting on the heels. The hands rest lightly on the thighs. In other arts, meditation is done in a cross-legged position. The length of a meditation session may vary, from a moment to several minutes to much longer. In some styles, notably the Indonesian arts, tests may include long hours of silent meditation, sometimes lasting up to several days. When faced with a long period of meditation, the student may torture himself or herself with fears of failure or discomfort, thinking *How can I sit for so long?*

I'll go crazy! Then again, he or she may be able to find a profound peace and stillness. These long sessions teach the student that the mind can be of great service in keeping the body ready and alert, and that sometimes one's worst enemy is oneself.

The angry man will defeat himself in battle as well as in life.
— samurai saying

LETTING GO

—

Many feelings come up during training. Sometimes, practice is fun and feels great. At other times, it is boring and frustrating. Sometimes students get angry. All the feelings possible in the world arise in the training hall.

When such feelings arise, the experienced martial artist lets them go. An angry fighter won't win a fight, because he or she will be unable to concentrate. A frustrated student won't progress.

But when difficulties arise, it can be hard to let them go. The meditation trick of "emptying one's cup" can help. The student's mind is like the cup. When feelings arise, the cup fills to the brim. Bubbling and brewing with anger or self-doubt, the cup is so full that nothing else will fit inside. Soon the cup overflows, and all that results is a big mess.

So when feelings come up in training, the student can instead empty the cup — visualizing the cup turning over and the feelings spilling out, then seeping deep into the earth and disappearing. An empty cup means there is room for learning and most important, room for the student.

The Story of the Okinawan Samurai

A poor Okinawan fisherman once borrowed money from a Japanese soldier. When it was time to pay his debt, the fisherman hadn't a cent. Angered, the samurai drew his sword.

"I have started to learn karate," the fisherman said in protest. "And the first thing I was taught was never to strike in anger." The samurai was so surprised to be reminded of his first training vow that he let the fisherman go.

That night when the samurai returned home, he found another samurai sleeping beside his wife. He was bursting with anger and once again drew his sword. But the fisherman's words echoed in his head: "Never to strike in anger."

The samurai left the house, then returned loudly and called to his wife from the doorway. He was met by his wife and, to his surprise, his mother dressed as a man. The women had been bothered by intruders, and his mother had dressed like a samurai in order to frighten them away.

The next month, when the fisherman came to pay his debt, the samurai refused his payment. "Keep your money," said the samurai. "It is I who owe you."

KATA PRACTICE

—

A *kata*, sometimes called a form or a set, combines fighting spirit and technique into a choreographed series of movements. Most karate and kung fu styles include standard forms, sometimes as few as one or two, sometimes as many as thirty or more. Designed to show speed, concentration, power, and beauty, the *kata* is a personal expression of a martial artist's training. Each form tells the story of a particular fight against imaginary opponents. To the observer, the martial artist should convey the intensity of a real fight. Breathing, focus, and spirit come together in a well-balanced form.

The most important role of forms practice is to get inside the art and to become one with the movements. Through repetition, the practitioner brings more and more of himself or herself to the performance. Every kick is broken down and precisely executed. Each *kiai*, or shout, is timed perfectly. Even the eyes focus on the imaginary attackers. After a good *kata* performance, an observer could swear that there was an actual fight!

In most kung fu and karate styles, forms are practiced at every stage. Beginners use forms to learn basic techniques. Intermediate students gain precision and focus through *kata* practice. Advanced students work toward achieving the blissful state of being immersed in the movement. Beginners usually prefer fighting to forms practice until they realize that *kata* practice creates the arsenal for sparring. A good fighter mixes kicks, hand strikes, and blocks into a smooth, spirited flow of movement. A *kata* champion is a formidable opponent.

HAND STRIKES

—

The punch is the most common hand strike. A proper punching fist is formed by rolling the fingers up tightly. The thumb folds across the first two fingers and is never tucked inside the palm, where it could be trapped and easily broken. To strike with this fist, one must be careful to keep the wrist flat from knuckle to forearm.

Using this fist, there are several ways to strike. The reverse punch is one of the most common. To begin a reverse punch, the fist rests, palm up, at the waist. One then thrusts the fist from the hip, turning the palm over just as the fist makes contact. This twist, the "reverse," adds power to the punch. It is important that the wrist stay flat. Contact is made with the first two knuckles. The fist is drawn back to the waist after impact.

The vertical punch, the back fist, the hammer fist, and the uppercut also use this basic fist position. In some styles, a punch is pulled back quickly after contact in a whipping motion, much like the snapping of a coiled towel. This pullback creates a powerful strike without requiring the martial artist to be exceptionally strong.

palm-heel strike

bird's fist

hammer fist

knife hand

Many styles use all parts of the hand for striking, not just the fist. In a strike called a ridge hand, the thumb side of the knuckles is used in an extended position to make contact with the head or face area. In a knuckle snap, the second knuckles are used in a whipping manner to "snap" an opponent. The fingers are placed together and focused into a point to create the beaklike bird's fist, which targets the eyes or vital areas.

The base of the hand can be pushed upward into the throat or nose. This palm-heel strike is a basic self-defense move. The classic "karate chop," with fingers held tightly together, actually uses the area near the base of the wrist to make contact. This strike is also called a knife hand.

knife-hand strike

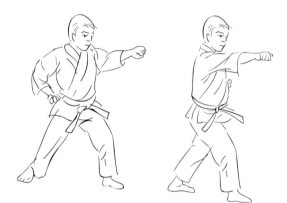

reverse punch

palm-heel strike

back fist

KICKING
TECHNIQUES
—

The most common kicks are the side kick, the front kick, and the roundhouse or circular kick. These kicks go by different names in each style, but in all styles, they must be performed correctly and swiftly in order to be effective.

A good kick begins with a good windup position, called the chamber. For front and roundhouse kicks, the student first stands with one foot ahead of the other so that the body is balanced. The chamber is created by raising the kicking leg at the knee. The knee cocks high, and the foot flies out. The student then pulls the knee back to the chamber position before returning the foot to the ground or kicking a second time. The chamber provides the focus needed to strike with power.

Surprise is also an important quality in a kick. From the opening stance, with one leg in front, a kick may be executed with either the forward or rear leg. Sometimes a student will signal what kind of kick is coming, telegraphing his or her intention, by taking his or her stance in a certain way or by making anticipatory motions. Telegraphing is like calling ahead to inform one's opponent of the attack. An observant fighter will see the kick coming and be ready with a block. Hours of training can help stop telegraphing and strengthen the element of surprise.

Targeting the groin, the head, or vital organs, different styles use strikes with the top of the foot, the ball of the foot, or curled toes. Depending on the kick, a pivot, or turn, of the standing leg may be necessary. Pivoting is essential in throwing a roundhouse kick. Stomping is also an effective variant of kicking, especially against a fighter who is on the ground.

If one falls, most kicks can be thrown from the ground. A roundhouse kick is effective from a sitting position, targeting the legs of the opponent. An ax kick is another excellent ground technique, best used against another grounded fighter. It looks just like its namesake; the leg comes up and falls straight down, with the heel striking the target.

In some styles, particularly tae kwon do, high kicking, targeting the head or chin, is the ultimate goal. In other styles, one never kicks above the waist. The low-kicking styles developed in places where it was difficult to balance, such as on wet, snowy, or rocky terrain, where going to the ground was the smartest fighting strategy.

Kicking is best done from a distance of several feet. If your opponent is too close, it is difficult to chamber correctly. In close-range fights, striking with the knees or elbows, or executing low stomps are good alternatives.

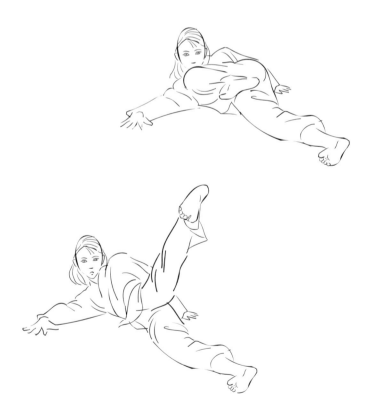

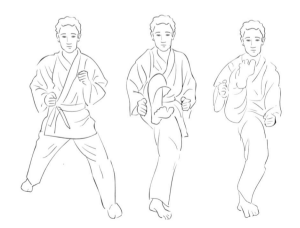

STANCE TRAINING

—

Animal stances, such as the cat stance, horse stance, and crane stance, build strength and balance. As in ballet, with its basic leg and arm positions, or baseball, in which the batter learns to stand a particular way, most martial arts use basic stances from which other movements occur.

The horse stance is one of the most typical. Students train to hold this position for longer and longer lengths of time. A good cat stance, with most of the weight on the back foot, gives the martial artist a springboard for other techniques. A crane stance comes in handy if a practitioner is kicked in the leg or has one leg swept out from underneath him or her. Eventually students practice moving from one stance to another, such as from tiger to cat to crane.

BLOCKS AND PARRIES

—

Each style teaches different blocking and parrying techniques. Most styles use the hand or fist to block hand strikes; others use the elbows to parry oncoming hand strikes or kicks. The upward block shields the head, and the downward block redirects a kick. Yet the hands and arms are not the only blocking tools. Each body weapon, including legs and feet, can be used to block as well as to strike. A knee can be raised to thwart a kicking attack. A foot parry is a quick kick to the ankle, stopping the opponent's kick before it has a chance to happen.

Wrapping the leg of an opponent is another way to block. As the attacker moves in with a kick, the opposing fighter steps toward the kick, reaching under the knee, then wrapping the leg tightly to his or her own body. The attacker is then vulnerable to being swept, felled by a sweeping movement of the blocker's leg aimed at the attacker's standing leg.

A good fighter works blocking and striking into a smooth flow, so that every block moves to a strike and is as fierce as an offensive move. A powerful block damages as much as a strike and deters further attack.

A Million Times

A legendary teacher once taught one of his prize students to punch. The student put his fingers together in a fist and hit the target a few times.

"Can you teach me something else?" the student asked.

The teacher frowned. "First practice the punch a million times," he told the student sternly. "Then I will teach you something new." The student was discouraged, and went in search of a new teacher.

The new teacher taught the student a kick. "Practice a million times," he said.

"What? Not a million times!" The student once again went to find a new teacher.

The third teacher taught a basic block. "Practice a million times," the teacher said, and left the dojo.

The student was really upset. "All this practice!" he muttered. He did try to practice a little, but he was soon bored and left the school early.

The next day, the teacher asked how his practice session went. "I practiced very hard, Sensei," the student said. "Just as you asked, I did the block a million times. I am ready to learn something new."

The teacher smiled and nodded. Then, as quick as lightning, the teacher raised his fist and brought it down a hair's breadth from the student's head. The student's hair fluttered! The strike was so fast that the student hadn't even had time to think of blocking.

"Practice a million times," the teacher said, leaving the student by himself.

That night over dinner, the three teachers laughed about their precocious student. Years later, when the student became a master himself, he told the story of the young martial artist who tried to trick his teachers. "Practice a million times," he told them. "I will know."

To train properly, a technique is practiced over and over and over, until it can be done without thinking. After some amount of practice, the student begins to learn how the technique works. Soon the technique emerges almost by itself. The body knows to move without the mind telling it what to do, like an animal that instinctively reacts to danger or a pianist whose fingers fly across the keys with ease. This meeting of mind and body takes years of study.

The journey of a thousand miles starts from beneath your feet.
— Lao-tzu, TAO TE CHING

Kiai!

Unseen power can lift heavy loads.
—I Ching

The *kiai* is the shout associated with martial artists. A Japanese word, *kiai* translates as "spirit meeting" or "energy focus." Different arts use different sounds, but the *kiai* always works to bring spirit to the moment of impact. During the *kiai*, the muscles in the abdomen tighten, putting more power behind the strike. A *kiai* also helps when getting hit. Tight stomach muscles coupled with a swift exhalation of air protect the internal organs and bring energy to the part of the body under attack.

A strong *kiai* can also scare or rattle a sparring partner. In a close fight, a loud *kiai* can startle an opponent and give a martial artist the winning edge. Sometimes the *kiai* is short and loud; at other times it is long and drawn out. Many Chinese masters are able to stun animals with the power of their *kiai*.

The *kiai* is the outward representation of *chi*, or vital energy. The sound of the *kiai* comes up from deep in the belly, from the center of the body where *chi* is stored. Pairing a *kiai* with a block or a strike unifies body, mind, and spirit.

Some *kiai* do not use sound. Sometimes called tiger's eyes, a silent *kiai* is a concentration of energy that travels through the eyes. A fierce look can stop or stun an attacker before he or she gets close enough to strike.

The Legend of the Stone Tiger

A long time ago, a young couple were walking in the forest. It was a beautiful day, the sun was shining, and the breeze whispered in the trees. The couple were very much in love, and very happy.

Suddenly a tiger leapt from the bushes and attacked. The two young people struggled, but the woman was fatally injured. The tiger escaped into the forest, and the young man wept as his partner died in his arms. Full of grief and anger, he vowed to kill the tiger.

Each day, the man went into the forest with his bow and arrow and spent hours searching for the tiger. Early one morning, he spotted the beast sleeping under a tree on the far side of a meadow. He placed an arrow in his bow, drew back, and let go. The arrow soared high across the meadow and pierced the tiger's back. The tiger lay still as the man excitedly rushed toward it. To his dismay, he discovered his arrow stuck in a striped rock!

Although the man was saddened, the villagers were impressed that he had shot an arrow into a stone. No one had done this before, not even the most accomplished bowman. They urged him to do it again. But although the man tried hundreds of times, he could not repeat his feat.

This story is the basis for the Japanese saying "A strong will can pierce a stone." In order to pierce the stone with an arrow, the man had to believe with his whole being that the stone was actually the tiger.

It is the same in training. Success—be it breaking boards, winning competitions, or doing the best kick you possibly can—depends on believing in oneself with one's whole being.

TRAINING
EXERCISES
—

You may train for a long, long time, but if you merely move your hands and feet and jump up and down like a puppet, learning karate is not very different from learning to dance. You will never have reached the heart of the matter.
— Gichin Funakoshi

Training differs from style to style. But in every art, training exercises are done without chitchat and with complete focus. Practicing with targets or in pairs teaches cooperation. Helping one's fellow students do their best is a big part of training. By holding a target steadily, one helps one's partner work to his or her capacity. Putting everything into practice ensures that everyone works to his or her highest potential.

Whatever the training task, there is always something to learn. Even students standing in line waiting to kick a target can practice concentration. While holding a target, one can study the telegraphing of other students.

In some arts, such as *poekoelan* and *capoeira*, one can practice drumming and singing even if one is injured and needs to sit out during practice. Something is always learned even by watching other students train.

CHRISTINE BANNON-RODRIQUES

Christine Bannon-Rodriques started training in karate at the age of thirteen because a friend asked her along to a class. "At first, I was an average student," she claims. "I was nothing special, but I really loved training."

It was four years later, after she earned her black belt, that she started to set higher goals. "I thought, if I can earn a black belt, what else can I do?" she explains.

Christine set her sights on the northeastern championships, and after many hours of hard work, found herself carting off gold trophies. Next she conquered the nationals, sweeping the gold in three categories: fighting, forms, and weapons. After that, she tackled the world championship. Again, she was a three-way winner!

Her victories led her to Hollywood, where she worked as a stunt double in *The Next Karate Kid*. She is currently starring on the TV series *Quest for the Dragon Star*.

Bannon-Rodriques also passes on the karate tradition to her hundreds of students. To make sure her students are well rounded, she requires an okay from parents and teachers before students can test for their next rank. "Setting goals in karate helps kids in everyday life," she says. "Doing well in school or deciding what you want to do when you grow up—all this is the same process as going through the belt system. If you work hard and take one step at a time, you will succeed."

The Tests of the Shaolin Monks

The legendary abilities of the Shaolin monks suggest that training at the temple was no piece of cake. After fifteen or more years of training, a monk was considered ready to test to become a master. By then, he would have demonstrated, in his daily conduct, that he was compassionate and gentle and knew how to restrain himself from violence.

Testing began with hours of written and oral exams on history, philosophy, and religion. Physical testing came only after these mental and emotional exams were completed successfully. In a test designed to challenge both awareness and fighting skills, the monk had to make his way down a long hall filled with booby-trapped weapons, such as knives, swords, and arrows, rigged to strike when least expected. As he navigated this maze, the monk also had to fight off fellow students, both armed and unarmed.

At the end of the passageway, the monk faced his final adversary: Blocking the exit was a huge, heavy ritual urn full of hot coals. As the monk embraced the urn in order to lift it, the marking on its sides—a dragon on one side and a tiger on the other—were burned into his forearms. For the rest of his life, the monk wore these brands as his certificate of graduation.

BELTS AND SASHES

—

The Shaolin monks did not wear colored belts tied around their robes. But belts or sashes, introduced by Japanese martial artists, are fairly commonly used in modern training to indicate rank.

Each art uses a different system of ranking, and some do not allow belts of any kind. Some Chinese martial artists, such as those who train in t'ai chi and *wushu*, rarely wear belts or sashes but often practice in beautiful silk training suits. Some styles, such as those from Indonesia and Thailand, denote rank with bright sashes, which are more in keeping with their country's traditional dress.

As interest in the martial arts has increased in the United States, some traditional styles that never used belts before have started to award them because American students are encouraged by progression through the ranks. In the Indonesian art of *poekoelan*, students usually wore a white sash until they were considered black belts. This process might require ten years of hard work! Since students got discouraged without recognition for their efforts and dedication, colored sashes are now earned at each stage of training.

In most systems, belts and sashes are presented only after a student undergoes a test. In some schools, tests are extremely difficult, and students are pushed to the limits of their skills. At testing, a student may be asked to perform everything he or she has learned to that point. Commitment and dedication are judged, as well as attitude. A student who is full of himself or herself or displays bad attitude may not pass the test even though his or her physical skills are excellent. Students must show good character and respect, and not just act like fighting machines.

Tests may also judge endurance. A black belt test can last two or three days. Some of the time is spent in meditation, while the rest is spent displaying physical skills. Black belt hopefuls must fight several attackers both in the school and in a natural setting such as the woods. During the test, the student may be asked to clean the training hall, the teacher's house, and even run ten miles. If the student is open, accepting, and willing, his or her attitude will bring success.

How Long?

Once upon a time, a young boy traveled across Japan to study with a famous teacher. When he arrived at the dojo, he was met by the sensei.

"What do you want from me?" the master asked.

"I want to be your student, and I want to be the best in the whole country," the boy replied. "How long will it take?"

"Ten years or more," the master answered.

"Ten years!" The boy was surprised. "What if I study harder than any of the other students?"

"Twenty years," said the master.

"Twenty years! What if I practice day and night?"

"Thirty years," replied the master.

"Why is it that each time I say I will practice harder, you tell me it will take longer?"

"The answer is simple," the sensei said. "When one eye is on the result, there is only one eye left to find the way."

Better than Okay

After one difficult black belt test, a teacher asked a young student how he thought he had done. The teacher stood with the black belt looped across her shoulders, ready to tie it onto the tired student. The student stared at the belt. His legs ached. After a grueling two-day test, that belt would soon be around his waist!

"I did okay," he said. The teacher was surprised at his attitude. She thought he had done everything very well.

"Just okay?" asked the teacher.

"I could have done better."

The teacher took the belt from her shoulders and slowly folded it up.

"I need you to do your best," she said. "I will accept your best, whatever that is. But if you did not do your best, you don't honor yourself, or me." She tucked the black belt under her arm.

Several months later, that young man took the test again. He made sure he did his best, for the entire two days. Now a teacher himself, he expects his own students to do their best as well. At the end of testing, he always asks his students the same question his teacher asked him: "How do you think you did?"

His students always answer, "I did my best."

RANKING

Most martial arts use similar colors for ranking. Each color has a particular meaning:

White: *Innocence and Purity*
By wearing a white belt, the beginner shows a willingness to start his or her training fresh, with an open mind and heart.

Gold or Yellow: *Energy and Light*
The student is now energized by training, although his or her energy, like that of the sun, is not yet harnessed.

Blue or Purple: *Deepening Understanding, Looking Toward the Blue Sky*
The student is beginning to realize the vastness of the art, like the open blue sky. Purple is also symbolic of bruises!

Green: *Growth in the Art*
Like a tree, the student is growing tall.

Brown or Red: *Rooted in the Art*
The tree's branches are now grounded by a strong trunk and network of roots. The student has created a firm foundation from which to proceed to the next rank.

Black: Black symbolizes the depth of the student's knowledge, and also the mystery and power of the rank. Only one out of every one thousand students earns a black belt. Although most people think a black belt is the ultimate achievement, attaining this rank marks the beginning of real training. There are many degrees of black belt, as many as ten in some styles. In Japanese styles, these are called *dan*. A Japanese stylist with a first-degree black belt is called a *shodan*.

Over time, a black belt starts to wear thin. With continued training, the threads of the white cotton begin to show. Eventually the entire belt turns white! This change is symbolic of the return to innocence and purity. It is a reminder to the advanced student to keep a beginner's mind and stay humble. It is also a warning to those students who think earning a black belt makes them hotshots.

Ultimately, any color belt or sash reflects one's willingness to learn, show respect to the teachers, and do the hard work of training.

WEAPONS

—

The martial arts use hundreds of types of weapons, ranging from the highly forged blades of the Japanese swordsman to the practical farm tools of the Okinawan peasants to the beautiful but deadly Indonesian fan.

Weapons training usually starts after training in basic empty-handed techniques. To begin, students use wooden, plastic, or other fake weapons in order to learn without injury. Once a student has shown an understanding and respect for the weapon, he or she may advance to using the real thing. Weapons are never wielded in anger or in jest.

Okinawan Farm Tools

Tonfa: A short stick with a handle, this Okinawan weapon made from the handle of a millstone was originally used for grinding rice.

Kama: A three-foot-long pole with a curved blade attached, the *kama* was originally a sickle for cutting rice. It is a difficult weapon to defend against; its curved edges can chop, slice, block, and hook. Often, two *kama* are used at the same time, one in each hand.

Nunchaku: Once used by Okinawan farmers to beat rice, in skilled hands, this weapon is deadly. It is made of two sticks twelve to eighteen inches long, connected by a rope or chain. *Nunchaku* are used in a twirling motion for blocking, striking, choking, or catching the weapon of an opponent. Bruce Lee works this weapon beautifully in the film *Enter the Dragon.*

Sai: This three-pronged forklike weapon was traditionally used in the planting of seeds. It is often used in pairs.

Staff Weapons

Staffs and Spears: Popular in many arts, these weapons are generally about six feet long and made of wood. Staffs, called *bo* in Japanese, are used to stab and block. Spears are tipped with cutting blades and may be used to slice. Either can also be twirled to prevent an attacker from approaching. And striking and thrusting with both ends gives the person skilled in these weapons many offensive options.

These sticklike weapons developed from the branches used by farmers to carry baskets of food or water on their shoulders. When attacked, the farmer would drop his cargo and wield the stick as a weapon.

Halberd and Naginata: These staff weapons with axlike blades have been used for many centuries. With ends that can be used for cutting or stabbing, they were effective against opponents wielding swords as well as those on horseback. Samurai women were especially skilled with the *naginata*, a seven-foot-long weapon with a curved blade two to three feet long. *Naginata-jutsu* is popular among modern Japanese women and is practiced as a competitive sport. A Chinese variation of this weapon is called a *kwan tao* or *quondo*, and the Korean version is called a *bong.*

Swords and Knives

Katana: the traditional sword of the samurai, with a blade twenty-four to thirty-six inches long

Broadsword: Sometimes wielded in pairs, light versions of this classic Chinese weapon appear in many modern kung fu styles. The single-edged sword is held with one or two hands. In martial art forms, the blade is used mainly for thrusting, slashing, and cutting.

Bokken: a wooden practice sword about three feet long, also effective as a fighting weapon

Kodachi and Wakizashi: Japanese short swords with blades between twelve and twenty-three inches long

Tjaluk: one of the hundreds of Indonesian curved-blade weapons

Specialized Weapons

Whip Chain: Used in many Chinese arts, the whip chain is swung overhead and in front of the body, both for blocking and striking. Up to twelve feet long, this weapon is unpredictable and in skilled hands is deadly. The Japanese use an iron weight or pick at the end of the chain.

Urumi, or Spring Sword: Used in India by the practitioners of *kalaripayit*, this weapon is a deadly mass of steel blades. Usually kept in a coil, when drawn and swung, the sword blocks an attacker from getting close. To stop the sword, the fighter catches the blades safely around his waist.

Shuriken: An iron disk with three to eight points, this weapon, also called a throwing star, was used by the ninja. A skilled person can throw a *shuriken* accurately up to thirty feet. The ninja carry nine *shuriken* because nine was their lucky number.

Iron fan: This weapon sometimes has sharp pointed tips, which, in the past, may have been dipped in poison. The fan is a beautiful and deadly weapon used by women in martial art forms resembling traditional dances. It is popular in Chinese and Indonesian martial arts styles.

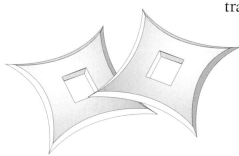

Weapons are the tools of fear;
a decent man will avoid them
except in the direst necessity.
—Lao-tzu, TAO TE CHING

ADVANCED
TRAINING

—

Power of mind is infinite; power of body is limited.
—Koichi Tohei

Traditional masters hold back one or two advanced techniques from even their most skilled students. Only when the master has chosen the special student who will carry on the art after his or her death will he or she reveal all the information he or she knows.

In ancient times, training was a lifelong commitment. A single task could take ten years to learn. This was especially true for the advanced skills that involve the combination of spirit, mind, and body. Supernatural powers attributed to masters of the past were actually techniques that took years and years to accomplish.

Using the fabled Chinese Red Sand Palm technique, a master was able to injure an opponent from a distance of several feet. To learn to do this amazing feat, first the student worked on a fistful of sand until he could grind it to dust. Once able to dissolve the sand in his palm, the student worked to develop intense concentration. It was said that just stepping toward the sand with the full intention of grinding it could make the sand melt into powder! According to old masters, after years of practice, the Red Sand Palm expert was able to crush iron balls from a distance. Eventually this powerful energy

can make himself so heavy he is difficult to budge. Then, when he is ready to be picked up, he will actually feel lighter! At her black belt test, nine-year-old Sui-yin Yuen grounded her energy and could not be lifted by five men.

Today, many students practice breaking boards and bricks as a way of furthering their training and developing this kind of mind-body power. Some students crush stacks of five or more bricks with a single blow. Others shatter ice with a butt of the head. At tournaments and special events, practitioners demonstrate walking on broken glass, holding fire, and lying on nails. To prevent injury doing these sorts of things, it is necessary to be an advanced student with strong powers of concentration, for these kinds of achievements can be accomplished only with intense focus and *chi* power.

could be thrown toward an attacker standing several feet away.

Learning to leap over cars, sleep standing up, and walk without leaving footprints are skills that take many years to develop. Although some people think these feats are merely special effects or trickery, there is documented proof that such things have been done.

Children instinctively know how to use *chi*. A child who does not wish to be picked up

Training in the martial arts includes not only intense physical conditioning but challenging mental discipline as well. Practice in the martial arts may span a lifetime or just a few months. Whatever its length, training includes learning about and being committed to the traditional spirit of the arts. This spirit includes honoring and respecting one's teachers, one's training partners, and most of all, oneself.

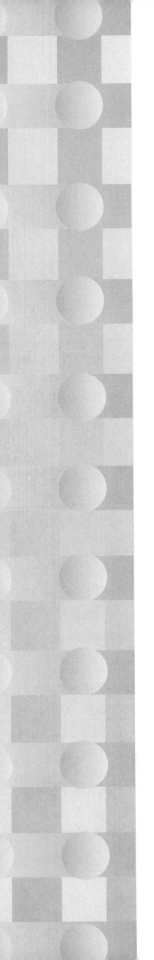

Part Four

—

MARTIAL ARTS AND YOU

—

*When you are content to be simply yourself
and don't compare or compete,
everybody will respect you.*
—Lao-tzu, TAO TE CHING

Martial arts schools are spreading across the United States at an amazing rate. As people from other cultures move to America, they bring with them rich and exciting traditions. Over the last forty years, even some of the most secret martial arts systems have been brought from Asia to the United States, giving Americans a wide choice of styles.

Some people fear that this new openness will water down the arts. The old masters who taught for food and clothing on the grounds of religious temples are nearly all gone. Commercial schools that emphasize belts and winning tournaments may alter the face of karate and challenge the true spirit of the arts. In the past, students had to prove their commitment and good intention before they were allowed to train. Nowadays, schools open their doors to most anyone who can pay for lessons. Some practitioners are concerned that deadly techniques will fall into the wrong hands.

The only hope for the survival of the martial arts is through physical training and the commitment of teachers who believe in the heart and soul of the arts. Good teachers see the spread of the arts as a path for people to better themselves and bring about a peaceful world.

Today's children will grow to be tomorrow's masters. If you train hard, one of those masters might be you!

WHAT'S RIGHT FOR YOU?

—

Whatever the guru teaches, it will add up to only one quarter of that student's knowledge. A quarter he derives from his own personal interest, and from hard work; a quarter comes from God's blessing, and the final quarter comes in his old age from his own personal experiences.
—Vasudevan Gurrukal, master of the northern style of kalaripayit

When choosing a style to study, you should consider what type of training you want to do. Do you want to learn an acrobatic art such as *wushu* or a slow, steady art such as t'ai chi? Maybe you want an art that includes music and dance, such as *capoeira* or *poekoelan*. If you want to learn self-defense, make sure the art teaches practical moves that can be used on the street in dangerous situations.

Before signing up, be sure to observe a class. Does it look like the students are enjoying themselves? Can you understand what the teacher is saying? Does the teacher make sure everyone is safe? Watch both beginning and advanced classes to see if the style and teaching method agree with you. Some areas offer many styles to choose from, so observe several classes before deciding. If you live in an area where there are no commercial martial arts schools, check out your community center, YMCA, or a local community college to see if classes are offered through these institutions.

Be wary of commercial schools that ask that you sign a long-term contract up front. To begin, sign up for only a month. Take into consideration dues and enrollment fees, and ask about additional costs, such as charges for testing or mandatory uniforms. Many schools have scholarship funds or work-study programs for students who are unable to pay full dues.

All true martial arts styles have the same goals. It is important to get a style suited to your body and to the kinds of things you want to learn. Most important, you need to feel comfortable in your school and with your teacher.

TOURNAMENTS

—

Sport karate is practiced all over the world and now is an Olympic event. Karate tournaments help to popularize martial arts among children and also provide a place where serious martial artists can judge the effectiveness of their techniques. Unlike what you see in the movies, tournament fighters do not fight to the death. On the contrary, the main emphasis in tournaments is on form and control.

A karate tournament includes three events: forms (*kata*); weapons; and sparring or fighting (*kumite*).

Kata are stylized combinations of movements that resemble a fight, although the opponent is imaginary. A student demonstrates the form to the best of his or her ability, with full power and intense focus. The movements are precise, the *kiai*, or shouts, loud and direct. Most tournaments include a musical event in which *kata* are performed to rock or pop music.

The judges should feel as though the form reflects a real fight. They score the performers from one to ten, looking for accuracy, balance, difficulty of movement, and spirit. Does the competitor look like he or she is totally involved in the *kata*? Are the eyes focused? The *kiai* strong? Presentation is extremely important. The competitor is watched from the moment he or she steps into the twenty-by-twenty-foot ring. Is he or she confident? Nervous? A good sport?

The competitor first addresses the judges, saying his name, rank, style, and the name of his *kata*. Then, with the judge's permission, the competitor steps back into the center of the ring.

Using all the concentration he or she can muster, the student begins with a bow. At this point, the judges are watching for focus and for heart, the love and devotion to the art demonstrated by a sincere bow.

The student then explodes into movement. The *kata* is performed full out: kicks, punches, spins, flips, and blocks. At the end, another bow. Then the student waits, in a ready stance, eyes alert, for the judges' decision.

"Judges call!" yells the center judge. The score cards are shown. Points are recorded. The student bows once more to acknowledge the judges before stepping out of the ring and returning to the line of competitors waiting their turn.

After all the competitors have performed, the judges call out the first five places. The winners line up before the judges and bow again before receiving their prize of a trophy, medal, or plaque. Some black belt competitors receive cash awards. A smart competitor always shakes the judges' hands. That judge may be at the next tournament, and students want to leave a good impression!

The weapons event is performed much the same way as the *kata*. Competitors demonstrate their ability to wield knives, whip chains, *nunchaku*, or spears accurately and with finesse. As with forms competition, the weapons event is performed alone, with each competitor showing the weapon in the context of an imaginary fight.

Sparring is entirely different. Competitors are divided into groups by age, rank, sex, and sometimes weight. Beginners fight against beginners, intermediates against those similarly trained, and black belts against each other. Men and women are sometimes divided by weight so that size is not a factor in the outcome.

Wearing padded equipment on head, hands, and feet, competitors line up at ringside and are paired arbitrarily. As they enter the ring, they bow to the center judge and to each other. They then line up, facing off with several feet of space between them. There are usually three judges, at the corners of the ring. At the judges' shout, the fight begins.

When the first targeted strike hits, the judges stop the fight and make their decision as to who gets a point. Sparring competitors have to follow strict rules about target areas and the level of contact acceptable. Beginners may not make contact to the head or face areas, and most tournaments score only for hits above the waist. Excessive force or poor sportsmanship is grounds for disqualification. Because there is often a flurry of activity, it is sometimes difficult for the judges to agree on which competitor got his or her technique in first! The first competitor to get three points within a two-minute time limit wins the match. This person advances to the next round of fighters until the last two face off for the final challenge.

Competitions are good practice for testing out skills, both physical and mental. The nervousness and fear one feels before going into the ring is similar to that felt in many situations one is likely to encounter in life—school presentations, oral exams, job interviews—not to mention self-defense situations out on the street. Learning to stand in front of others, do one's best, and feel good about oneself whether one wins or loses is an important part of the spirit of karate.

A FAMILY AFFAIR

Satisfaction lies in the effort, not in the attainment. Full effort is full victory.
—Gandhi

Sensei Joseph Catlett is understandably proud of his student Syreeta. At eleven years old, she consistently places high in competitions and has won many trophies. She is the youth reporter for a national magazine, the *Martial Arts Gazette*. And she is also his daughter.

Sensei Catlett is the founder of the Katsuru system, which stresses the principles of discipline, respect, compassion, and love. His students compete in tournaments in order to learn about themselves. "There is really no loser in competition," he says. "Through competing, one learns that improving oneself as a person is the most important thing in life."

Syreeta and her *sensei* are not the only family members who train in Katsuru. Two years ago, inspired by his sister's dedication and successes, Dyrwen, sixteen, started training and has been steadily improving ever since. A cousin, Gregory, fourteen, now trains with the family as well. His first love is football, and his martial arts training has greatly improved his skills on the field. Cousin Joven, at ten, is the youngest member of the Catlett family team.

Team Catlett trains hard, with the belief that self-improvement and staying positive and healthy are the most important reasons for studying a martial art. Meanwhile, the Catlett School of Combat Arts in Philadelphia is filling up with trophies!

DISABLED MARTIAL ARTISTS

—

As in the garden, some flowers stand taller, while some rest on the ground. All are beautiful.
—old saying

As Linda wheels herself into the cool *dojo*, her students run to line up against the wall. She is wearing a *gi*, with a black belt tied smartly around her waist. Her arm muscles ripple as they push against the wheels of her gleaming silver wheelchair. Paralyzed from the waist down, Linda has been training in karate for more than ten years and now teaches.

Her disability makes it difficult for her to kick, but her hand strikes are precise and strong. And with the aid of her hands, she is able to firmly connect her feet to a target or an opponent. She is also able to maneuver her wheelchair so that it works like a weapon. Those who fight her say that getting close enough to strike is difficult. "She's a tough fighter," says one of her teammates. "Her punches are strong, and that chair really hurts when it hits your shins!"

Linda is just one of a growing number of martial artists who have physical challenges. Many people who are blind, deaf, or have other disabilities have found strength and confidence through training. Some tournaments now include events for disabled students. Training in self-defense can be particularly important for people with disabilities, because they are sometimes seen as vulnerable and targeted as crime victims.

Alex, a blind student, found that his keen hearing helped him develop skills other students lacked. In one class, his teacher had the students practice with the lights off. Alex was comfortable in the dark and was able to hear the attackers before they reached him.

Every student is able to express his or her inner beauty through training. All students are capable of challenging themselves to improve their skills. Although many people train to learn self-defense or to better their health, every martial artist is ultimately training in order to express, understand, and better themselves. More so than perhaps any other sport, martial arts are for anyone.

Live so that people will want your autograph, and not your fingerprints.
—John Corcoran, martial artist and writer

When to Fight, When Not to Fight

In his autobiography, Gichin Funakoshi, the father of modern karate, tells a story of his early training. Once, during a train ride, Funakoshi saw a drunken man bothering other travelers. The man became mean, and it looked like he would become violent. Funakoshi watched and planned his techniques, imagining all kinds of holds and punches. He readied himself for a fight.

Suddenly an old man sitting in a corner by himself spoke to the drunken man. "Do you prefer wine or sake?" he asked.

"Huh?" The drunk was caught off guard.

"Do you drink wine or sake?"

"Uh, wine!" the drunk replied, still trying to look mean.

"Wine! Why, I love wine! What kind do you drink? Come sit with me and talk about wine."

The drunk was taken with the old fellow's friendliness. He took a seat and was soon crying and telling the old man his troubles. Funakoshi felt terrible. He thought of the ways he had imagined hurting this poor drunken fool. Right then, he knew that fighting should never be chosen as the first option.

SELF-DEFENSE

—

I have the right to defend myself!" chant the children at One With Heart, a martial arts and self-defense training center in Portland, Oregon. The students there are taught verbal and physical self-defense skills by black belt Karin Kruse. They are taught about home and phone safety and how to deal with people who want to hurt or injure them.

A central focus to the training is that kids have rights. For instance, no one has the right to touch them in private areas. They also learn how to defend themselves against kidnappers. An older male student acts like the "bad person" and tries to convince a young girl to come to his car. The girls responds in a loud voice: "No, leave me alone. Get away from me!" She starts to run for help and as she does so, she shouts, "Help, this man is not my father! Help!"

In another situation, the man picks up a boy from behind. The boy yells, kicks, and shoots his arms into the air. He slips to the ground, out of the man's grasp. Running away, he yells for help. The class cheers him on.

Self-defense training also helps when other kids try to pick a fight. Through role playing, two boys practice stopping a fight before it starts. One twelve-year-old boy approaches a younger boy on the school playground. "I hear you do karate," the older boy says. "Let's see what you can do!" He puts up his fists.

"No, I don't want to fight," the smaller student says.

"C'mon. What are you, a sissy? A wimp?"

"Leave me alone," the student replies. He walks away, signaling that he would get help from a teacher or an adult. The other kids agree that the aggressive boy looks like a bully.

The message Kruse gives is always the same: "Never start a fight. Use your karate to defend yourself or those you love."

At the end of class, the students sit in a circle and recite affirmations: "I am a strong and powerful kid!" "I have the right to say no!" And the always popular "Not all adults are right!"

Three Principles

Sensei Linda Ramzy Ranson is a second-degree black belt in the art of Fuji Ryu *jujutsu*. She is an exceptional teacher of self-defense for women and girls. She helps women understand that they have choices. "Women can fight back not only to defend their basic right to a safe and free living space," she says, "but also to maintain the high degree of self respect to which they are entitled."

Sensei Ramzy Ranson has formulated three principles for self-defense, which she lives by and imparts to her students:

1. It is better to know it and not need it than to need it and not know it.

2. Any decision you will make to survive is the right one.

3. Fight with conviction, and do whatever it takes to survive.

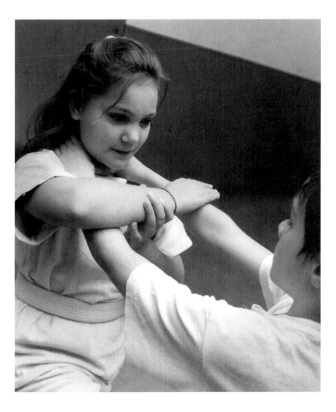

A Modern Code
of Honor

—

Just like in the days of the samurai, today's martial artists strive to live up to certain standards of behavior. Sifu Kate Hobbs teaches martial arts and self-defense to at-risk kids at Project DESTINY, in Oakland, California. DESTINY stands for De-Escalation Skills Training Inspiring Nonviolence in Youth. Sifu Hobbs has developed a Warrior's Code, a list of characteristics that she feels describes the true martial artist:

Love: A warrior is skilled in body and kind in heart.

Respect: A warrior respects herself or himself and all living things.

Care: A warrior believes that caring for herself or himself means caring for our world.

Responsibility: A warrior takes responsibility for his or her actions and makes a superior effort in all situations.

Honor: A warrior uses fighting skills honorably, only to protect herself or himself and loved ones. A warrior never raises his or her fists in anger.

Peace: A true warrior lives by this code and firmly believes that the greatest warrior is the one who stands for peace.

The Warrior's Code works in life as well as in training. "In this time, when everything is so crazy in front of us, we need a basis for living," says thirteen-year-old student Sam Mende Wong.

Nine-year-old Andre Harris puts it this way: "The Warrior's Code teaches you to respect people no matter what they say to you, and to respect yourself enough to ignore them even if they're messing with you."

Samurai Self-Defense

A violent mind wields a careless sword.
—Miyamoto Musashi

One day, on a crowded river ferry, two samurai from different clans sat facing each other. One had been drinking and was loud and obnoxious. He tried to pick a fight with the other samurai.

"So," he barked, "can you use those swords, or are they just for show?"

The other samurai sat calmly and smiled.

"I challenge you to a match! Show your skills!" The drunken samurai rose and started to prance around with his sword. The boat rocked terribly, and the other passengers drew back, no doubt worried about the consequences of a sword fight on such a small, crowded boat.

"I need not fight with my swords," the other samurai replied, still sitting. "Nor do I fight with my hands."

"Ha!" the drunk said, thinking he had an easy match. He lunged toward the other samurai.

"I will take your challenge," said the sober samurai, swiftly rising and evading the grip of the other. "But let us get on dry land, away from these innocent bystanders."

"Fine, fine," said the drunk, grinning from ear to ear.

The boatsman pulled the ferry to a small beach. Immediately the drunken samurai jumped out, drawing his sword.

Just as quickly, the sober samurai pushed the boat away from the shore.

"What? Where are you going?" the drunk yelled, and started after the boat. He stumbled in the shallow water. "Get over here! You accepted my challenge! Get back here and fight me!"

"This is how you fight without swords or hands," the samurai said.

The cries of the drunken samurai amused the passengers as they floated away into the distance.

MARTIAL ARTS IN FILM

—

Whether filmed in Hong Kong or Hollywood, martial arts movies continue to wow audiences and whip up interest in training.

Although he has been dead now for more than twenty years, Bruce Lee is probably still the most famous martial artist action hero. On the heels of Lee's fame, Chuck Norris moved into the spotlight. As a young soldier stationed in Korea, Norris studied the Korean art of *tang-soo-do*. He returned to America full of enthusiasm and began teaching in the early 1960s. By winning numerous competitions, Norris made a name for himself. After years of acting classes, his dream of starring in Hollywood movies finally came true. Norris has now starred in more than twenty movies.

Steven Seagal, an aikido master, shares top box-office billing with kick boxer Jean-Claude Van Damme. Both are accomplished martial artists who have spent years in the training hall. Even more popular are the television characters the Teenage Mutant Ninja Turtles and the Mighty Morphin Power Rangers. At times, these shows reflect the true spirit of the martial arts.

Currently Hong Kong stuntman, director, and actor Jackie Chan is breaking into stardom as a martial arts hero. Already popular and well known in Asia, Chan's recent films are beginning to be released in the United States. Chan is known chiefly for his daring. Jumping into fire, swinging from ladders, or riding atop a moving train, Chan prides himself in performing every stunt in his films. "I want people to leave the theater saying, 'Jackie Chan was great,' not, 'The special effects were great.'" Chan is also extremely funny and brings a comic aspect to his action star roles.

Canadian Elvis Stojko brought the martial arts into the limelight at the 1992 Olympics—as a figure skater! Stojko wowed audiences and captured the silver medal with his "*kata on ice*." He skated to the theme music from *Dragon*, the movie about the life of Bruce Lee, and his routine incorporated many martial arts techniques. A double black belt in kung fu and karate, Stojko continues to work hard and pursue a higher level of martial training.

MICHELE "MOUSE" KRASNOO

Champion Mouse Krasnoo began training at the age of eight, but she was so small that she looked five. She earned the nickname "Mouse," and it has stuck with her ever since. "My *kiai* sounded like squeaks, and I was so little," she explains. "I was the only girl in class, and I was scared. But I stuck with it."

At twenty-one, Krasnoo is now well known on the karate circuit and was seen in the movie *Kickboxer IV*. A film major in college, she wants to be an action movie star. In addition to gymnastic classes, and hours and hours in the studio, she also studies acting. "There are no female stars in action movies," she laments. "I hope to change that."

Having traveled to South America and Europe to demonstrate and compete, Krasnoo finds time in her busy life to teach kids at her father's karate school. "Not everyone is a champion," she says. "The goal of teaching is to build character. A lot of these kids don't have anyone there for them at home. They need attention, and we try to give it to them."

The Wise Old Woman

A Story from the Indonesian Martial Art of Poekoelan

Once upon a time, a wise old woman lived high up on a mountain. All the children in the town below would go to her and ask questions, and she always knew the answers. Always! After a time, the children grew weary of her always knowing the answers.

"I know how to trick the old woman," one boy said. "I'll catch a bird and hide it behind my back. Then I'll ask the old woman, 'Is this bird dead or is it alive?' If she says dead, I'll open my hands and let the bird fly free. If she says alive, I'll break the bird's neck and the old woman will be wrong!"

The children laughed. They were delighted with the plan. They were finally going to trick the old woman!

So the boy caught a bird, and the children followed him up the mountain.

"Old woman," the boy said. "If you're so smart, tell me what I have behind my back."

"That's simple," the old woman said. "You have a bird behind your back."

"Yes, old woman, but tell me, is this bird I have behind my back dead or alive?"

The children held their breath. Had he fooled her?

But the old woman smiled. "That, my son, is in your hands only."

125

Each student of the martial arts has the power to choose what to do with his or her knowledge. In the right hands, the martial arts are a beautiful expression of physical and mental abilities and an outward show of admirable self-discipline.

Today's martial artists descend from spiritual people committed to a peaceful world. Those of us training today can strive to follow in the footsteps of the honorable Shaolin monks.

Your spirit is the true shield.
—Morihei Ueshiba

BIBLIOGRAPHY

—

Chow, David, and Richard Spangler. *Kung Fu: History, Philosophy and Technique*. Burbank, Calif.: Unique Publications, 1977.

Crompton, Paul. *The Complete Martial Arts*. London: Bloomsbury Books, 1992.

Draeger, Donn F. *The Weapons and Fighting Arts of Indonesia*. Rutland, Vt.: Charles E. Tuttle, 1972.

Fields, Rick. *The Code of the Warrior: In History, Myth, and Everyday Life*. New York: HarperPerennial, 1991.

Funakoshi, Gichin. *Karate-do: My Way of Life*. Kodansha International, 1975.

Nelson, Randy F., editor. *The Overlook Martial Arts Reader: Classic Writings on Philosophy and Technique*. Woodstock, New York: Overlook Press, 1989.

Reid, Howard, and Michael Croucher. *The Way of the Warrior: The Paradox of the Martial Arts*. Woodstock, New York: Overlook Press, 1995.

FOR FURTHER READING

⸺

In addition to the many books available on the history and philosophy of the martial arts, there are hundreds books describing the specific techniques and applications of each style. These books are mainly found in martial arts supply stores, or they can be ordered from the many mail-order companies listed in the major martial arts magazines. In addition to timely articles about a variety of arts and self-defense methods, these magazines often include interviews with action stars, provide in-depth information about training exercises, and list up-to-date information on tournaments and competitions.

Books

⸺

Hayes, Stephen. *The Ninja and Their Secret Fighting Art.* Rutland, Vt.: Charles E. Tuttle, 1981.

⸺. *Ninja: Legacy of the Night Warrior.* Santa Clarita, Calif.: Ohara Publications, 1985.

Hinton, William, and D'arcy Rahming. *Men of Steel Discipline: The Official Oral History of Black American Pioneers in the Martial Arts.* Chicago: Modern Bu-Justu, 1994.

Hyams, Joe. *Zen in the Martial Arts.* New York: Bantam, 1979.

Rafkin, Louise. *Streetsmarts: A Personal Safety Guide for Women.* San Francisco: Harper/San Francisco, 1995.

Reid, Howard, and Michael Croucher. *The Fighting Arts.* New York: Simon and Schuster, 1983.

Webster-Doyle, Terence. *Facing the Double-Edged Sword: The Art of Karate for Young People.* Middlebury, Vt.: Atrium Press, 1988.

Wiley, Carol A. *Women in the Martial Arts.* Berkeley, Calif.: North Atlantic Books, 1992.

Magazines

Aikido Today
Arete Press
P.O. Box 1060
Claremont, CA 91711-1060
(909) 624-7770

Black Belt
P.O. Box 16298
North Hollywood, CA 91615
(800) 760-8983

Inside Kung-Fu
4201 Vanowen Place
Burbank, CA 91505
(800) 846-8575

Journal of Asian Martial Arts
Via Media Publishing Company
821 West 24th St.
Erie, PA 16502
(814) 455-0629

Karate/Kung-Fu Illustrated
Rainbow Publications
P.O. 918
Santa Clarita, CA 91380
(805) 257-4066

Martial Arts Gazette
P.O. Box 187
Port Hueneme, CA 93044-0187
(805) 986-8425

T'ai Chi
Wayfarer Publications
P.O. Box 26156
Los Angeles, CA 90026
(213) 665-7773

FOUNDATIONS AND ASSOCIATIONS

National Women's Martial Arts Foundation
P.O. Box 4688
Corpus Christi, TX 78469-4688

Nine Gates Institute
6052 Wilmington Pike #231
Dayton, Ohio 45459

United States of America Wushu-Kungfu Federation
6315 Hartford Road
Baltimore, MD 21214

United States Judo, Inc.
P.O. Box 10013
El Paso, TX 79991

United States Taekwondo Union
1 Olympic Plaza, Suite 405
Colorado Springs, CO 80909

INDEX